Octave

Octave

Essays on Waldorf Education

by

Magda Lissau

AWSNA

Printed with support from the Waldorf Curriculum Fund

Published by:
The Association of Waldorf Schools
of North America
Publications Office
65–2 Fern Hill Road
Ghent, NY 12075

Title: *Octave*
    Essays on Waldorf Education
Author: Magda Lissau
Editor: David Mitchell
Copy Editor and Proofreader: Ann Erwin
Cover: Hallie Wootan
© 2007 by AWSNA
ISBN # 978-1-888365-80-1

CONTENTS

Prelude

In the course of my many years as a Waldorf teacher, and as one who was honored to help aspiring teachers develop towards becoming Waldorf teachers, I have been conscious of the many extraordinary individuals I have had the opportunity to know. One aspect of my experience has become quite remarkable, as, in the course of working in several countries on three continents, I was privileged to meet a few of those special teachers who had met Rudolf Steiner. They were fully involved in what I would like to call the stream of Waldorf education.

This stream of Waldorf education was conceived by Steiner and some of his early students as the means to bring about social change in the world at the end of World War I. Social change comes about slowly but surely as the consciousness of human beings transforms and progresses. In my first years as a teacher in St. John's School in the Camphill Schools, Aberdeen, Scotland, I met several of these special individuals. Later on, in the Netherlands, and still later in Johannesburg, South Africa, I met yet others.

I experienced myself to be inserted in a mighty river, a streaming impulse, toward changing humanity. In this stream of flowing awareness towards social change there are some islands, islands of concepts, personified by individuals. I would like to bring out in these pages the streaming and transforming force towards the goal of changing consciousness of society at large, which may also bring individual fulfillment. May readers of these pages feel themselves part of a rising stream towards the future of humanity.

Each of the following essays was written with some of the questions in mind that aspiring Waldorf teachers have asked me in past years. While there are many books on Waldorf teaching and the Waldorf curriculum, I felt that some questions could be put into greater perspective to round out the picture of Waldorf education as helping humanity towards its further development.

A word about the title: An octave completes a scale beginning with the tonic. As a melody rises, individual thinking capacity drives it further. Consequently the distance of the septime towards its completion in the octave requires quite an individual effort. These pages are dedicated to the many who strive towards the completion of this individual effort in order to guide their students towards an appreciation of what is needed for real progress in today's world. So may these words inspire confidence in the task of bringing humanity forward as hoped for by Rudolf Steiner.

As in the preparation of my past books, I appreciate the care that David Mitchell and many others have spent in getting this selection of essays ready for publication.

– Magda Lissau
August 2007

Motivating Children and Adolescents in the Classroom

The structure of this essay follows Rudolf Steiner's well-known designation of the seven levels of will as described in his *Foundations of Human Experience.*[1] These will be described and then analyzed according to specific principles which will be outlined at the end of the essay. Throughout I have applied various suggestions from my forty years of class teaching in Waldorf schools on three continents.

I. Instinct

The first level of will as described by Steiner is the level of *instinct*. "We can study instinct only when we see it in relation to the form of the physical body."[2] He precedes this comment by comparing the human body with those of animals. What is the connection between human bodies, animal bodies and the instinctual urge? In brief, most instinctual urges are based on bodily needs—hunger, thirst, sex, sleep, mothering instinct, and so forth. All these mentioned we share with the higher animals. One instinctual urge, however, is uniquely human, though researchers in recent years have been somewhat successful in training primates in something similar: imitation. In the case of primates, however, imitation does not develop into actual intellectual knowledge. A wonderful and remarkable capacity of small children is imitating parents in gesture, word, attitude and so forth. While this capacity continues into later life, we are less likely to use it as adults.

This capacity of imitation is the basis for much that children younger than school-age learn about the world. It is a capacity directly bound up with perception. Perception is based on the sense organs of our physical body. Consequently Steiner's observation that instinct has to do with the physical bodies of humans, and also other mammals, is borne out. As adults we tend to underestimate the strong sense perceptions made on young children. As adults most of us have learned to shut off perceptions when they become too overwhelming, strident or intrusive.

Children have not yet developed the capacity to defend themselves against the visual, audio and tactile intrusions of present-day advertising and the media. They easily become prey to these. One technique of self-defense on the part of children is to imitate these strong impressions. So if a small boy pretends he is a truck and careens around the room, vrooming and turning a pretend steering wheel, that is his way of humanizing, absorbing and digesting portions of the sense perceptions which come on too strong for many little people. Or if a girl playing with dolls puts her doll through what her mother demands of her precisely, this is clearly a case of the child working through these demands on herself. Gender-oriented roles are commonly impressed in young children early on.

The capacity of imitation, based on an instinctual urge, is of tremendous significance in the developing of learning in the following way: Through our imitation of external sounds, words, actions, and so forth, we impress these into our memory. In effect we train our memory, which in young children of preschool age is the beginning of, but not yet a complete, purely mental memory capacity. While the first reaction of preschoolers is to play out the observed event in bodily activity and repetitive words, actions, even sing-song, eventually this process will become something purely mental. It is vital to realize that when imitating, particularly if the imitation takes place at a later time, the experience and perception of the event that is imitated is abstracted—that is, separated out—from its physical occurrence. It had to become purely mental in order to be imitated and placed into memory. To begin with, repetitive actions as imitations of external happenings reinforce memory. Aligned with this is the capacity of human beings to designate themselves by saying "I."[3] This ability is also based on memory and imitation. Toddlers and infants call themselves by their given name as addressed by their parents. As soon as they can say "I," an important phase in the establishment of memory has been reached. From that moment on, children begin to experience a continuity of existence: while experiences vary, the "I" continues every day.

A further capacity of early childhood related to imitation, sense perception and, thus, the physical body is the capacity for play. In playing, the child handles materials he knows through sense perception, playfully arranging and rearranging them over and over. This playful change in organizing the perceived world is a manifestation of fantasy, or imagination. The capacity of young children to employ fantasy in play marks the beginning phase of freeing the mind from the physical reality of perceptions and its object-bound constraints and playfully rearranging this reality. All learning in later life is based on this capacity of the human mind to abstract external reality, replace it with symbols—signs, words, and so forth—and manipulate these symbols in coherent ways. Hence the vital importance for adults to give preschool age children the opportunity to experience free play, free play as opposed to play organized by adults.

Let us examine briefly several possible hindrances to a pure and living experience of instinctual urges. If children were to be denied playful expression, their memory development could be thwarted, and there might be consequences to their learning capacities. Much of early childhood play involves physical action. The urge to imitate instilled in children is most frequently played out through bodily actions. If a child were restrained, denied the ability to move her or his limbs freely when following inner impulses of imagination, and sit, for instance, in front of a television where the only action would be eye action, then memory development would be undermined. If, on the other extreme, a child were given complete freedom, with no recurring moments (rhythm) in her or his daily life—such as meals, bedtime stories, and so forth—then there might be harm done also. Unfortunately there is a tendency among adults today to consult children at too early an age about what they would like to eat, to do, where to go, and so forth. Children need structure in their lives, as adults do too.

The times of the day, as well as the seasons of the year provide a natural structure for our lives. Physical materials give us natural limits, as does our physical body give us a natural structure, not only in terms of strength, but also in terms of reach and capacity. Little would it help to rail against the limitations of our bodies. But within the structure of our bodily capacities, we may develop agility, strength, endurance, skillfulness of small and large muscles, powers of observation, and so forth. We may develop these to the best of our abilities within the framework of our given structure—that is, our body. Similarly a structure in our daily life can give us form.

On this first level of will it is nature itself that gifts human beings with instinctual urges. These need not be enhanced, neither suppressed; it is, however, helpful for growing up with the best of our bodily gifts that these very gifts are fostered in natural ways. It is therefore vital that the natural urge to play, involving physical bodily activity, is not buried. Individuals, when reflecting on themselves as adults, may want to become clear how these instinctual urges influence their actions.

II. Drive

The second stage of will is *drive*. "When you speak of drive, you speak of something expressed uniformly during the entire time from birth until old age." What might that mean? A compelling urge to move towards a specific goal. Steiner brings drive into connection with each human being's web of life. Is he saying that each individual has a certain amount of energy, of will, to move along the path of life? Does this mean that there are differences among individuals of the energetic application to one's life's tasks? There is the implication of movement in the word *drive*. We move towards something all our lives, although not always aware of the aim. At times we move listlessly; at other times we move energetically; at still other times we are *driven* towards something, not always aware of what that is. One might also say that we are driven from birth on towards what will be eventually our moment of death.

In a remarkable film made recently in the Antarctic by Luc Jacquet, *The March of the Penguins*, Emperor penguins are filmed walking, or sliding, on a seventy-mile trek over the ice to their breeding grounds. What drives these creatures? During the Antarctic winter, when eventually the eggs are laid, then the fathers protect them under their thick feathers, while the mothers trek back to the ocean to feed themselves and bring back food for their chicks, who have hatched in the meanwhile, and for the fathers, who have not had food for four months. To view this extraordinary animal behavior is to see a physical depiction of the nature of *drive*. Drive literally drives our life energies.

Another characteristic of drive, in its relation to the life organism of human beings, is in connection with the life processes as described by Steiner.[4] These life processes work on in human beings, and also in animals, in an automatic manner, but can, at times, be interrupted and controlled by the will of the individual. This, however, is extremely rare. Think of breathing, the first life process. Of course, we are able to hold our breath when diving underwater, but only for a short time. A brief review of these seven life processes will help to clarify what *drive* actually is.[5]

The life process of breathing is continuous, from a child's first breath at birth to a human being's last breath before death. The life process of warming, that is, adjusting one's own warmth in relation to outside temperature, is also continuous. An interesting example of adjustment is given in the abovementioned film. The Emperor penguins are an interesting example of this, huddling together during severe winter storms. Moreover, there is a group-awareness, because the ones on the outside of the huddle regularly change places with the ones in the middle—to preserve the warmth of the whole group. The life process of nourishing may seem intermittent. There are times when we choose to fast for a reason, although ultimately we need to feed our bodies. Looking again at the example of the Emperor penguins, the fathers guarding and warming the eggs do not feed for about four months—unimaginable for human beings—certainly driven by the foremost urge to protect their offspring. The life process of secreting is not so easy to observe, as in human and animal bodies numerous glands constantly secrete a variety of necessary enzymes and other digestive substances. The life process of maintaining obviously takes place in all living creatures, plants as well as animals and humans. The same with the process of growing. There are time constraints upon the life process of reproduction; we see this urge in human beings begin at puberty, and, in women, ending at menopause. In most mammals there are seasons when they are in heat. In human beings there are times of the month when a woman is most likely to conceive. In penguins the drive towards reproduction is so great that tremendous obstacles are overcome in marching towards their breeding grounds. We can witness this drive in other animals as well—from turtles and whales to salmon, and so forth.

This second stage of will—drive—can be easily exploited. For instance, advertising uses the sex drive to sell goods, and movies use the death drive to sell horror pictures. Charities are successful in raising money because most of us are ready to help needy individuals. Not that helping others is wrong, but the means employed are at times questionable. All the life processes, as they drive our daily existence, may be abused by overstatement or by denial. A further enticement to individuals in our present time—not that similar enticements were not available in ancient times—has to do with the drug culture. Fear of legal or health consequences or the lure of out-of-this-world experiences determines our relationship to a variety of drugs, all challenging an individual's capacity of self-control. Politics exploits daily these two parts of our soul life, and frequently we are taken in by this exploitation. Of course, any individual reacts differently to danger, fear and the promise of excitement.

On this second level of will it is still nature that gives human beings the gift of drive. It is up to individuals to recognize whether any drive must be modified, for ethical or societal reasons. Again, human self-examination will tell the individual what is right.

III. Desire

The third level of will is described by Steiner thus: "When you speak of *desire*, you speak of something created by the soul, a momentary creation… it arises then fades away. Thus, we can see desire as something more closely connected with the soul than simple drive."[6] It is far more difficult to differentiate in the human soul which aspects are affected by desire, and this presents a problem for modern psychology. When comparing animals to human beings, it is clear that animals exhibit instincts, drives and desires, but no motives. Motive is the fourth element of the human will and will be described in the next section.

Desire is an element that drives a great deal of our actions. When considering desire as it is carried in each individual by the astral body, one has to bear in mind that the human soul is the carrier of our mental capacities to think, to feel and to will. Consequently the realm of desire is divided into these three areas of experience. At times these overlap. Fleeting in nature, desires arising and waning in the shadow world of the soul may become stimulants to actions. These actions may be rooted in thinking or in feeling, or in the will itself.

Desire as It Affects Thinking

Desire enters readily into our arena of thinking, for instance when we are keen to gain information, knowledge or wisdom. In this arena thinking is also connected to drive, that is, to the life organism of human beings. This desire for knowledge is naturally imbedded in all human beings, but the kinds of knowledge desired are varied. There is a vast difference in the pursuit of knowledge by a scientist, by an intelligence officer, or by a person seeking religious enlightenment. The whole range of what Steiner describes in his exposition of the threefold social order as the area of the free spiritual life is encompassed by the possibility of desire for knowledge.[7]

Desiring knowledge is a fundamental trait of the human mind. Human beings do not necessarily believe that there are limits to the knowledge they may gain, despite the declarations of philosophers and scientists, past and present. When we are able to see the implications of knowledge, as well as its applications, we are often inspired by the fiery wish to learn more. And there are ethical considerations. How will we make use of the knowledge we gain? Shall we use it in a pure way, or with self-serving intent? Shall we serve humanity at large or just ourselves, or maybe a group interest only? In this area of knowledge we are faced already with moral questions that require considerations of our conscious self—the ego.

Many actions taken by human beings are driven by a desire for knowledge. At times these actions are justified for the sake of knowledge, or the advancement of human knowledge; however, these may be harmful to others, or destructive of nature, as for instance in the testing of substances on animals to ascertain harmfulness to human beings.

The wider implications of the harmfulness of certain aspirations or pursuits of knowledge, or intelligence, or information, is at present quite apparent. When abuses of prisoners held by the U.S. military in Iraq, Afghanistan, or Guantamo Bay are reported, these are often excused by the urgent need for information. During the Cold War, the most intricate devices and interrogation techniques were used in order to get information for both sides. Here, of course, is an example of desire, which is judged valid and important for national security, but which leads to inhumane actions. It is important to view this issue not only from a group perspective, but also from the perspective of individuals, who are ultimately held responsible for their actions, and should therefore develop a moral and ethical stance.

Human desire is stirred up with the goal to get individuals to buy whatever is being sold: Pictures are often presented to inflame egotistical and selfish desires. Where, for instance, would the fashion industry be without such pictures? Or politics? And so forth. The human intellect, when infused with desire, can very easily rationalize the validity of these desires. Such rationalizations are often at the depths of our souls, possibly not at a conscious level, to persuade us into action. We must strive to be conscious of the fact that much of the desire nature works in us unconsciously, even within our reasoning capacity.

When attempting to stimulate students in their natural desire for knowledge, it is best to provide them with a variety of pictures, of which some should be incomplete, for then these invite questions. Questions about the known and the unknown are essential tools to awaken desire for knowledge. The moral and ethical responsibility of the teacher, or of any other adult in a position of authority, is essential, for pictures will provoke the desire nature and may lead to unfortunate actions on the part of students.

Desire in the Realm of Feeling

Feeling strengthens desire considerably. Moreover, desire in the realm of feeling carries a mood. Desires fluctuate—they make themselves felt, they appear, then die down, much as a whale may appear in the ocean, sounding, then submerging again. We are indeed living in an ocean of desire, navigating our way by internal and external compasses, and the moods are the winds by which we steer. Our external compasses are the conventions of society, within which we choose to stay or which we choose to ignore. Our internal compasses are our own moral and ethical convictions, which may, or may not, be in our conscious mind.

We will experience a wide range in the degree of desire. It may be too strong, too weak, or just fleeting. In our present time the advertising industry attempts to keep a desire burning all the time, to influence individuals by keeping their desires stirred up, so that the purchase of products will be continuous. In this case advertising attempts to counteract the natural life of desires that rise up and then die down again.

Desires lead to actions. At times these actions barely come into consciousness, at other times they prey on the mind for a long time. When the sudden impulse arises to purchase an ice cream cone, we usually do not give it much thought; we may curb our desire for a later fulfillment, or rationalize it, or give in to the desire. We do not normally investigate what has awakened the desire for ice cream. We might have heard a jingle that reminded us of the ice cream vendor of our childhood or another memory. This is an example of a fairly simple feeling and response to a desire.

Other examples may illustrate psychological problems. When we experience the setting of moods, often created by music, to underline pictures, we have a very potent force which may be difficult to resist. For instance, we might be under continuous tension because of unfulfilled desires, unfulfilled because they are irrational, misleading or seductive. By contrast, we may be void of desires and leading a kind of vegetative life, floating along the surface of the ocean of desire, without aim. In either situation, the individuals are unusual and potentially unsocial persons.

From the viewpoint of teachers, harmony of feeling desires makes the best learning climate. At times it is good to stir up the desire nature of students, then calm it again, in order to eventually create a harmonious equilibrium. A widening of perspective, or a narrowing of focus, a playing with the moods, also provides the eventual balancing of desires.[8]

Desire and Will

When desire becomes action, then the transference from desire into will is achieved. We have the potential as human beings to reason, to weigh up our desires and control our actions. We may allow our feelings to do this weighing up and then proceed forward into action, or we may bypass rational consideration or weighing the consequences and react with lightning speed.

It is important to consider when desire, like lightning from the clouds, strikes into action in our soul life and so circumvents logical considerations. Many a crime of passion comes about because of such a lightning strike of desire. In this case, our desire nature circumvents rationality and becomes reaction to an external stimulus. In many instances a reaction becomes a life saver; in other instances, it spells disaster; in any event, a reaction does not give an individual any time for conscious deliberation.

Our desire nature may be compared to our internal weather. We may experience a sunny day and a blue sky, or we may experience storms. Whatever the inner weather, it is quite a challenge to control. It will be our ego, our essential self, that will be in charge of desires, and then we are not drifting in an ocean of desires, without direction, without support.

When dealing with children, we are often faced with either uninhibited desires or a total lack of desires. "I am bored. I don't feel like it. I don't know what to do" is a litany known to every parent and teacher. Likewise is the child's desire to do everything at once. Our response must be tailored to the age of the child. Trying to rationalize with children under the age of nine or ten will not do much good. For the younger child a picture of future events might help to steer him from an undesirable path of action. An older child can be reasoned with. An adolescent should also be met with reason, but we need to understand that adolescents are prey to desires that rise with violent intensity in the ocean of their soul life, and they do not as yet have the adult capacity of weighing the consequences of actions.

A teacher is actually much in the same position as an advertising executive—she or he needs to make life interesting and stimulating to awaken the desire for learning, to stimulate feeling for a subject, and to rouse the will to activity. The vital component in a teacher's arsenal in dealing with desire in children, in order to steer them into the appropriate channels, is to make lessons as interesting as possible. Students usually respond well when their interest is aroused. However, moderation in fulfilling desires should also be presented to children and adolescents through the examples of adults, teachers, parents, role models. (It is unfortunate that many role models in today's world do not exhibit restraint, but the contrary, the unmitigated descent into the desire nature.)

IV. Motive

Steiner expresses the essence of *motive* thus: "Generally speaking, we refer to instinct, drive and desire when influenced by the 'I' as motive. So when we speak of the will impulses in the soul and in the 'I,' we speak of motives and know that, although animals can have desires, they can have no motives."[9] The essence of the human self, the "I," the individual spiritual entity, has a relationship to the three lower expressions of will, but it is distinguished by the capacity to become fully conscious of her or his motives for actions. When considering motive, we come to the heart of this essay, for our interest is in how to enhance the capacity in children's, adolescent's and adult's souls to realize their motives. In this paper, however, we are mainly concerned with children and adolescents.

Let us be quite clear about the distinction between *motive* and *desire*. If we are driven to act, possibly not being fully conscious of why we act, we are probably acting out of desire. When we are making ourselves fully conscious of the consequences, we are acting out of motive.

When attempting to determine what will bring about the transformation of an inner experience into action, especially when raising it into full consciousness, we need to become clear of the specific process, involving all three levels of soul life, the same three levels as already discussed in the area of desire, but now brought to individual consciousness. When we considered desire in the realm of thinking, we described that pictures often stir us to action; in the realm of feeling, we described feelings, or moods to influence actions; in the domain of will, immediate reaction to external stimuli. Instead of being experienced in a dreamlike and fuzzy state of mind, these three areas can be explored now in full consciousness.

Forming a picture is essential when dealing with a fully conscious motive in the area of the thinking soul. Such a picture naturally arises even before the simplest action comes about, although in most cases we are not fully aware of it, and thus it might be relegated rightly into the arena of desire.

In our soul life we may speed up, or slow down, our inner experiences. It is possible to have a flash of insight, a flash of intention, a flash of mood, or a flash of reaction. When we carry out a very simple action, what happens is that an inner picture of our coming action flashes across our unconscious soul life and is made into an actual, external action within moments. Steiner speaks of the impulse of freedom in our thinking and the impulse of love in our will.[10]

In order to understand the essence of our soul life, we need to consider the picture of the human being as Steiner details it in all of his works. The life of thought takes place in an entirely non-physical way, otherwise the will could not penetrate into it. Our thoughts are like pictures in a mirror. Because our thoughts do not have physical materiality, we are free to arrange them at will.[11] However, when transforming a thought, a motive, or an intention into external action and deed, the intention energizes our limbs and makes the thought into external reality in the realm of love.[12] In this way a thought, which may simply be a picture, becomes reality through our action when it flows into our limbs. Each human being is an integrated individual, consequently our soul life and our physical and life organisms work together, directed by our conscious self. Because the human being is a totality, however, that which is a picture of thought, entirely non-material and insubstantial, jumps over into the realm of metabolism, into our limbs and moves these towards an action, thus making the picture into external and physical reality.

Consequently, when we would like to motivate students in their thinking capacities, we need to put before them pictures. These pictures could elicit questions, they might be incomplete, or even faulty. But by practicing the visualizing of pictures of external events or of internal happenings, we empower students to employ their thinking capacities. These thinking capacities may produce an immediate flash of insight, or they might produce a result only after much cogitation. Whichever way, by beginning with a picture, we may so motivate students.

When motivating students in order to interest them in the respective subjects to be learned, it is essential that the teacher bring pictures that will elicit thoughts and questions. Moreover, when bringing pictures that will stimulate thoughts and questions, it is advisable that such pictures describe human beings in a general way or involve possibly one student in order to demonstrate a particular picture.[13] Particularly in the middle grades, but also in the higher grades, pictures will elicit a thinking response in students.

Steiner often mentions that one of the important qualities of modern human beings should be to have interest in other human beings and events in the world at large. Such interest could be awakened by pictures, and eventually be lived out in work engendered by love for human beings and humanity.

However, we shall also motivate students out of the realm of feeling if we are able to accompany pictures with a mood. For instance, when students are required to write an essay, a teacher might describe the required theme, but also set a tone, a mood to act like background music.

How does one set a mood? We may use all tools available to actors. We may use tools described by Steiner as the temperaments. In his lectures to the first teachers of the first Waldorf school, Steiner pointed out the different ways that temperament language could be employed to give depth, weight and substance to a story. He also indicated how temperaments may be used in the teaching of math processes to first graders, and, further, how this may elicit feelings for the form elements in drawing.[14] We may use our own language, gesture, mode of description, tone of voice, and so forth. It is important to set the right mood in order to motivate students.[15]

When setting a mood, we employ language in a descriptive way, we paint a picture with words, we learn that some characteristic forms of pictures carry within them a meaning that goes beyond words, and we learn to apply such meanings to the objects of the world around us. This is what is meant by temperament language.

Finally, motivating students might involve pressure from the whole group. Such pressure, for instance to ensure that everyone needs to be really quiet so that the whole class might be able to concentrate on the given tasks, that something greater is involved than just the individual. This is somewhat related to what Steiner describes about the path in the human soul between freedom and love. When succumbing to the pressure of the group, we do not freely submit but do so because we understand why it is necessary. We respond to the pressure of the group—or, one might say, submit to a law—out of love for the group. This appeal to an awareness of the common good is appropriate in many circumstances. Pressure is generated, based on an individual's awareness that she or he belongs to a group. This is the arena for social problems, for in many individuals today there is an intense wish to be an individual. But that wish is not satisfied when there is only group pressure. An individual seeks to stand out apart from the group, and much of teenage behavior patterns in today's world may be understood as such an unfulfilled attempt to become individual and to set him or herself apart from the group. On another level of social problems entirely, one might experience that members of certain groups feel themselves slighted by society at large, refuse to abide by group pressure and legality, and attempt to win special rights of their own.

How does one deal with this longing to become an individual? Instead of reacting to so-called individualism in manners of hairstyle or dress that are intended to offend adults, we need to encourage individual expression in interaction with a group-awareness. No small order for today's educators of teenagers. How does one create harmonious interaction between these two polar opposites—individualism and group benefits? The challenge for educators is to find means of expression and experience in which an individual is creative but still participates within a group. Among various possibilities there are two means that provide this opportunity: arts experiences and community service.

In many high schools it is a given that a few weeks a year are dedicated to *service learning*. I shall not go into detail about service learning, however, the arts provide an excellent medium for individual expression. Steiner's indications point quite clearly in this direction. Moreover, not only are the arts infused in every subject in the curriculum in a Waldorf school, but at the high school level an overview of the evolution of different arts is presented as a subject for intellectual study in itself.

The more they [the students] can be led to an appreciation of what is beautiful, the better will they be prepared, at the time of puberty, to tackle the practical tasks without being harmed for the rest of their lives. Only if at the right age the aesthetic appreciation of a painting or a sculpture is cultivated, can a pupil, later on, safely gain an understanding of how a tram or a railway engine works. This is a fact a teacher should fully bear in mind. But beauty needs to be seen as being part of life and not as something separate, not something that is complete in itself. In this respect our present civilization has yet to learn a great deal, especially so in the field of education.[16]

Steiner expresses that the experience of art, and the artistic-aesthetic judgment capacity that it wakens, leads to the capacity of understanding our present world. Moreover, we are in the sphere of soul experience where we are neither completely free as in our thinking, nor completely chained by external reality that determines our will, but *half free* as in our feeling life. "Fortunately, art is able to create impressions of something that is not actually there." [17]

When considering that students need to learn to relate to the world as it is, to its technology, to its political situation, we may engender the capacity of social responsibility by working with the arts. Some arts lend themselves readily to enhancing capacities for developing social conscience. In contradistinction to arts that must be practiced individually (such as architecture, painting and drawing), music, drama and eurythmy are social arts, for they foster group work and group experience. When engaged in such group efforts, individuals are encouraged and learn to forego *prima donna* actions and are usually willing to do their part so that the whole may be presented, much as playing a single instrument in an orchestra.

Beyond the level of motive, Steiner explains that the higher levels of will point to the future. Not only the future of human evolution, but also the future development of each individual human being. Steiner describes that the next three higher levels of will—that is wish, intention and resolution— only come to expression and activation after death.[18]

V. Wish

Steiner speaks of *wish* as a longing of each individual to have the opportunity to carry out a past action in a better way. In other words, this striving to do better becomes a wish that carries over into future incarnations. In this area, there is natural, and frequent, opportunity for teachers to instill in the student the wish to execute a specific task with better results in the future. In whatever major or minor task the wish to do better may be involved, this wish educates the conscience of children and adolescents, because in their souls they have a wish, as yet indistinct, to improve their performance.

If we look at the wider implications of such a wish, we are certainly dealing with ethical-moral issues in this respect. If a person is satisfied with her or his fulfillment of a task, then the aspiration to improve is absent. What is such an aspiration? It is a longing to go beyond one's present level of success. It is something that impels us to ever better and concentrated efforts. It has the effect of expanding ourselves beyond our present level of capacity. This is true in all fields of life, particularly in the realm of education and yearning for knowledge.

We are confronted in the area of wish with three distinct forms. One, as described above, is the ethical impulse to go beyond our present accomplishments, and so realize the wish, unconscious though it may be, to carry out a task better a next time. It is our conscience that impels us in this direction. The second possibility is that we do not feel any urge to do better, that we are entirely satisfied with the result, that we feel that *this is good enough*, and so we have no compunction to elevate our efforts. Often pride and arrogance hold sway in our souls in this second form of satisfaction. The third possibility is that we are never satisfied, always find fault with our results, and yet have no sense of what we really must do over time to improve. We become overly critical and judgmental of ourselves, and thus there is a self-destructive element which asserts itself in our soul. A kind of fear takes hold of us then. Of all three forms only the first one will allow human beings to strive for continuous improvement and to feel an inherent moral-ethical responsibility towards oneself and towards the products of one's work.

For teachers, at any level of kindergarten, grades and high school, as well as for parents, it is crucial to help children and adolescents to long for improving themselves, and so to help young people develop moral responsibility. How do we do that? One way is by comparing an individual's work with those of others, in a constructively critical way by emphasizing the goals. For instance: A map has been drawn by each student in the class. It was quite difficult, and it had to be done in a specific manner. After a few days we place all the maps before the class. We remind the students about the particulars of the task. Without naming the creator of each map, we ask for a show of hands for which map has fulfilled all the particulars. In this way, without being individually hurtful, it is clear who has really fulfilled the task to his/her best ability and who needs to improve. Names need not be named. A group judgment exerts a certain amount of objective pressure on an individual's conscience. The wish to do better is quietly encouraged and reinforced.

Group pressure, already mentioned in relation to motive, may also help when looking at the moral-ethical implications of the wish to do better. In the case of wish, it is far more subtle, because rarely do children and adolescents have a conscious awareness of this wish. Rather, they have an unconscious longing, which, however, contains a deep-seated conscience.

The intent and effort do so something better the next time is higher than regret. The wish echoes in this intent so that we may ask what it is that resounds as a wish. For those who can truly observe the soul, what resounds is the first intimation of everything that remains after death. What we feel is something of this remnant—namely, that we should have done better, that we wish we had done better. This form of a wish as I have just described belongs to Spirit Self... The other person who lives in you, the second person, always develops a clear picture (not as an idea, but according to will) of how to carry out an action should you again be in the same situation.[19]

As Steiner mentions in many of his lectures, it is vital to realize that one of the tasks of the present era, of the fifth post-Atlantean epoch, is to begin work on transforming our astral body into the Spirit Self. What is meant by this? The astral body carries our desire nature. When it is purified, it will become Spirit Self. In the course of earth evolution we shall make only the preparation for the development of this part of the human entity. As a preparation, our consciousness will not yet be in full control, but will still be directed by our self, our ego. But the capacity of Spirit Self to convey wisdom and morality to our actions may be carried by a group of human beings. By overcoming the selfishness of our desire nature as housed in the astral body, we gradually grow able to listen to our conscience and begin to sense the ethical implications to our actions.[20] It is possible that group awareness helps support individuals to act according to their consciences. Indeed, in many communities, such as religious communities of the past, such group awareness helped keep individuals from straying from the path. Of course, the present task of our fifth post-Atlantean epoch is to develop one's humanity beyond our own individual self, and now group awareness, awareness of what is beneficial for or detrimental to the further development of humanity, should, and does, become an active social force. Thus group awareness may already be the herald of Spirit Self, long before it will become available as an individual trait.

VII and VIII. Intention and Resolution

The next levels of will described by Steiner are *intention* and *resolution*. Both terms imply very conscious and deliberate consideration.

Deep in every person sits another person. In that other person a better person also lives, a person who always promises to do a completed deed better the next time. Thus, with each deed there is also a subtle and unconscious, a subconscious, intent to do the deed better in the next similar situation.

When we free the soul from the body, intent becomes decision. The intent lies like a seed in the soul; the decision comes later. Decision occurs in Spirit Human just as intent exists in Life Spirit and the pure wish in Spirit Self.[21]

In other words, Steiner links these higher levels of will with parts of the human being that are in the process of development and which provide the driving force for our experiences during the time in the spiritual world between incarnations. These forces lodging in the human will, with their connections to parts of the human being not yet developed, are the seeds of our next incarnation and prepare the possibility for us to repeat actions that were not done well, in whatever field of experience these may have occurred.

While here is not the place to speak of the transformation of a human being's soul in future phases of evolution, one might anticipate the directions this might take and find some relevance in some pedagogical situations. Two elements of human experience are destined for eventual conquest: fear and pain.

Fear as experienced in the soul seems to sap our strength, to hollow us out, to take our life. When determined to follow through with an intention, we frequently face obstacles and even danger. The determination to follow through with our intention, to overcome obstacles, to carry through despite opposition, strengthens our life energies. Have you ever experienced that the determination to carry out a plan despite opposition makes you feel more alive than had you succumbed to obstacles in your path? I believe that such an experience is a premonition of the future power of the Life Spirit which, according to Steiner, is the transformation of our life energies, our ether body.

Pain saps our existence even more so. Be it physical or in our soul, pain tempts us, even moves us to give up, to self-destruct. Suicide if often the result when an individual is overcome by pain. However, suicide is a denial of oneself. Pain is a challenge for our souls to learn. Individuals who experience pain and persevere, who are, so to speak, honed on pain, become very powerful in themselves and in their effect on other human beings. Think of holy men and women revered in all religions who have overcome physical or soul pain and thus have grown in their moral being to such an extent that they become examples to others and are able to help those who have not as yet attained their inner strength. These forerunners of humanity may be active in preparing the future Spirit Human, which is a transformation of the human body into a purely spiritual entity.

We may envision the future development of humanity in the transformation of our current physical and spiritual organizations by cultivating the several ideals as stated above. Overcoming pride and arrogance, fear and pain, which are learning tools to awaken the conscious ego, our spiritual self, are steps toward the future of humanity.

When teaching history, or just the stories of the first few grades, we have ample opportunity to give students examples of great men and women who have overcome obstacles, and so provide them with ideals toward which to strive. Of course, we may also give examples of individuals who abused their great gifts for selfish reasons, and so provide a contrasting picture of such ideals. In this way we may plant seeds for the future individual development of the students we teach.

You may have noticed that I have mentioned some aberrant forms for the qualities within the seven levels of will. The basis for these forms lies in what Steiner describes as the spiritual powers of Lucifer and Ahriman, who have substantial influence on each human being's soul life. Especially since 1879, it is evident that these powers have been thrust out of spiritual worlds again to take up an influential position in human souls.[22]

It is these beings who place obstacles in the paths of individuals who strive towards developing their innate spiritual potential. This resistance, which might be external and physical, or internal within the individual's mind and soul, will eventually work to strengthen the resolve of individuals in order to overcome these obstacles. When overcoming obstacles, a strengthening of the soul, of the self, takes place. While we may observe in our present time much misery and challenge for human beings in all areas of life, it is the intention of the spiritual powers to enable humanity to reach ever higher levels of their spiritual development.

> The most important contribution of art to the evolution of mankind is the training it provides for an understanding of future problems... In the epoch of the Consciousness Soul mankind must develop the capacity to comprehend man symbolically.... We must learn to perceive the spiritual archetype of man through his picture-nature. In future man will become to some extent transparent to his fellow man. The form of his head, his gait, will awaken in us an inner sympathy and understanding of a different nature from what we find in human tendencies today. For we shall only know man as an ego being when we have this conception of this picture-nature, when we can approach him with the fundamental feeling that what the physical eyes perceive of man bears the same relation to the true supersensible reality of man as the picture painted on canvas bears to the reality which it depicts. We must approach man in such a way that we no longer see him as a combination of bones, muscles, blood, and so forth, but as the image of his eternal, spiritual being.[23]

When we look at the soul force of will and its seven levels, we may begin to realize the challenges of human development as levels of achievement or advancement. When working with children and adolescents in a classroom setting, teachers may use motivation for work to strengthen the innate desire for doing well and doing good.

ENDNOTES

1. Steiner, Rudolf. *Foundations of Human Experience*, Lecture 4, Spring Valley, NY: Anthroposophic Press, 1996.

2. Ibid.

3. Steiner gives examples of how a child begins saying "I" to himself in *A Psychology of Body, Soul and Spirit,* particularly in the lecture entitled "Consciousness and the Soul Life," Spring Valley, NY: Anthroposophic Press, 1999.

4. Steiner, Rudolf. *The Riddle of Humanity*, Lectures 7 and 9 particularly, London: Rudolf Steiner Press,1990.

5. Another aspect of the life processes, as the foundation for the development of logic in the grade school years, is described by the author in her recent book, *Awakening Intelligence*, Fair Oaks, CA: AWSNA Publications, 2004.

6. Op. cit., Steiner. *Foundations of Human Experience*.

7. For instance, a selection of Steiner's ideas, edited by Stephen Usher, *Social and Political Science*, London: Sophia Books, 2004.

8. Many indications by Steiner deal with the harmonizing as well as the stirring up and calming down of desires as pedagogical instruments of class management. *Practical Advice to Teachers*, London: Rudolf Steiner Press, 1976, and *Discussions with Teachers*, London: Rudolf Steiner Press, 1983.

9. Op. cit., Steiner. *Foundations of Human Experience*.

10. Steiner, Rudolf. *The Bridge between Universal Spirituality and the Physical Constitution of Man*, Lecture 3, Spring Valley, NY: Anthroposophic Press, 1979.

11. Steiner demonstrates that it is not correct to say, "I think, therefore I am," as Descartes propounds, but instead we should recognize the non-material nature of our thinking and recognize that the picture nature of thinking is like a mirror without substantiality. Op cit., *Foundations of Human Experience*, Lecture 2.

12. Op. cit., Steiner. *The Bridge between Universal Spirituality and the Physical Constitution of Man*, diagram in Lecture 3.

13. Op. cit., Steiner. *Practical Advice to Teachers*, Lecture 7.

14. Op. cit., Steiner, *Discussions with Teachers* and *Practical Advice to Teachers.*

15. See the author's book on *The Temperaments and the Arts*, Fair Oaks, CA: AWSNA Publications, 2003.

16. Steiner, Rudolf. *Soul Economy and Waldorf Education*, Lecture of January 5, 1922, Spring Valley, NY: Anthroposophic Press, 1986.

17. Ibid.

18. I use different terminology than the translators use in the book *Foundations of Human Experience*, because I think that *intention* is clearer than *intent* and *resolution* is clearer than *decision*. Especially about the latter one could come up with several philosophical arguments.

19. Op. cit., Steiner. *Foundations of Human Experience*, Lecture 4.

20. Rudolf Steiner, *Intuitive Thinking as a Spiritual Path*, Hudson, NY: Anthroposophic Press, 1995.

21. Op. cit., Steiner. *Foundations of Human Experience*.

22. Steiner, Rudolf. *The Fall of the Spirits of Darkness*, Bristol: Rudolf Steiner Press, 1993.

23. Steiner, Rudolf. *From Symptom to Reality in Modern History*, Lecture 5, London: Rudolf Steiner Press, 1976.

Illustration, Imitation, Imagination

The sense organs in their subtle structures must become something different from what they used to be. What flows into the sense organs is what will gradually, and in a natural way, develop Imagination through the eye, Inspiration through the ear, and Intuition through the sense of warmth. Thus there need to be developed: imagination through the eye; inspiration through the ear; intuition through the skin.[1]

Observations

A master teacher visits the first grade in a Waldorf school. A superbly drawn picture, illustrating a story, is on the board. It might be drawn in colored chalk or on black paper. When it is time for the class to begin their bookwork, the teacher says, "And now, first grade, take out your crayons and draw this picture." She or he might have said, "Copy this picture." Later, when the teacher, together with the master teacher, look at the first graders' drawings, they are disappointed, for the famous imagination of that age of childhood is nowhere to be seen.

Alternatively, a master teacher goes into a class where the teacher has just finished telling an exciting story. The teacher concludes, "Imagine Johnny in the middle of the stream, holding onto his boat, with the treacherous trout jumping in and out of the boat. He is desperately trying to not overturn the boat, holding onto his oars, and skirting the rapids. What would you do? Now draw this in any way you like." When we look at these drawings later, we are stunned by their originality, power of color and movement.

Why did the students create stunning illustrations in the second scenario, but not with the first? In this chapter I hope to demonstrate the reasons for this difference. I intend to attempt elucidating some general principles, which, I hope, will be thought through and applied by individual teachers.

What Are Illustration, Imitation and Imagination?

ILLUSTRATION:

Illustration is ordinarily understood to mean: To depict in a drawing or painting composition the essence of a story or a historical event, whether actual or imagined. Its various aspects include:

- Technical drawing: To depict a natural object, a scientific process, or a technical process as exactly as possible.
- Geometrical drawing: To cleanly and clearly draw a geometrical construction, possibly coloring it to emphasize its particular features. This might be regular geometry or perspective drawing or the shadows of regular or irregular objects.
- Form drawing: To imitate correctly a form and reproduce it, either on paper with exact spacing and dimensions, or in any other shape. One should remark here that the letters and numerals represent forms to the child who is still learning to read and are introduced as such before becoming intellectual tools for conveying knowledge.

IMITATION:

Imitation is intimately bound up with exact observation through our senses, to copy as accurately as possible a given form, picture, gesture, speech pattern, or mode of behavior; or to read in imitation of another person's reading; to behave in imitation of another person's soul mood.

Imitation may take place in three-dimensional actions, but also in translating something that has been observed in three dimensions onto paper, that is, into two dimensions. There is an inherent activity of form and movement implied in such translations.

IMAGINATION:

Imagination is intimately bound up with the transformation of sensory experiences. Steiner describes this by linking imagination with sympathy, just as he links conceptual thinking with antipathy as clinical soul attitudes. He also links conceptual thinking with the nervous system, and imagination and sympathy with the blood circulation.[2]

- To imagine all of the above possibilities in detail
- Behavior patterns
- Real or possible events
- Scenarios of future events
- Forms of objects not found in the physical world
- Projected political and social structures, and so forth.

When Does the Distinction between Illustration, Imitation and Imagination Become of Vital Importance to Teachers?

The usual demands on students in a Waldorf school, requiring the above named capacities, could best be described thus: In kindergarten children will draw and paint largely in imitation of what they observe in adults. Generally speaking, their activity expresses what they see or experience in their environment. It should be noted, that kindergartners will not draw objects realistically. This is a capacity that will be developed throughout the grade school years. What children draw in early childhood comes basically in two forms:

- The younger children will draw using movements that are age-appropriate, and are quite typical,[3]
- Or they will draw their concepts of real objects, but these are, of course, not technically correct.

As a student advances through the lower grades, the *art of illustration* is taught early on to accompany the making of a student's own textbooks of their main lesson work (more on this later). One aspect is the learning of different painting and drawing *techniques*. This is done by imitation of the teacher's handling of crayon, paintbrush or pencil. Another aspect is the blending of colors, with crayon or pencil, as well as with liquid paint. Children often resist when blending colors as an aesthetic necessity and should be both encouraged and taught how to do so.

During the middle grades *technical drawing* becomes important to allow them to illustrate the natural world and later the world of science. By high school, the illustrative and technical capacities should be completely mastered by students, and then the *world of the great artists* is open for exploration. Their techniques are studied in detail. Learning various styles now becomes essential. Any student who intends to study to become an artist, in whatever discipline, will then continue her or his education in this respect.

Vision and Its Relationship to Illustration, Imitation and Imagination

When engaged in the visual arts, we are limited by what our sense of sight will provide to us. The visual arts include painting, drawing and sculpture. There are many media used for each of these. This paper will focus on the visual arts of painting and drawing.[4]

To begin with, in order to understand fundamental principles of teaching illustration, utilizing the capacity for imitation, and fostering the sense of imagination, we need to take a closer look at the human eye. The complexity of this organ is astounding. I shall point to only two aspects of vision which I believe are of importance for our understanding here: the capacity of focusing in on details, principally a function of the pupil; and the capacity for peripheral vision, largely a function of the edges of the pupil, leading towards the iris. This twofold nature of human vision is essential to understanding much related to the visual arts, but also to the process of learning to read. We may differentiate between (1) centering our vision, with intention and attention at a particular object and thus concentrating on focused vision, and (2) what peripheral vision is able to bestow.

In regards to peripheral vision, we may enter a different type of experience altogether, as if we were not quite fully awake and aware, but observe movements coming towards us from the periphery. Peripheral vision is usually hazy and not always colored. As soon as we notice something approaching us from the periphery, we usually turn towards it and focus our vision on it. In other words, it usually does not remain peripheral for long.

The focusing capacity is centered on a point in the eye called the fovea, a central place on the retina. To illustrate the difference between focused and peripheral vision, we could say that our focused vision is centered on a particular spot in the sky, say, the sun or the full moon, whereas the greater portion of the sky, where stars, clouds and other phenomena are seen, would be the equivalent of peripheral vision. Indeed, one might say that the happenings in the atmosphere, in the heavens, are like what appears to us in peripheral vision, from out of the circumference. Of course all this is also reflected onto the retina, but only on the periphery of the retina, not its center, the fovea.

A very basic experience, now going beyond the system of vision, is that of center and circumference, or focus and periphery. Steiner discussed this difference when describing the difference between our head forces and our limb forces.[5] We could say that the forces of the human head are concentrated on and akin to focused vision, whereas the forces of the limbs, reaching out into the cosmos, attune us to events approaching from the periphery and thus represent peripheral vision.

Similarly, we can relate these very different forces of head and limbs to the human psyche as well. We can regard focused vision in connection with the centralizing forces of the human head and connect peripheral vision with the limb forces, streaming out into the cosmos, and thus relating to the essence of vision in a very different way.

In this way we may relate focused vision, the centralized capacity to understand and conceptualize what is perceived, to what Steiner referred to when speaking about our nerves in relation to the forces of antipathy. We may relate the will forces in connection to the forces of sympathy and the forces invigorating human blood, with imagination and peripheral vision.

Steiner once commented that, when focusing on an object with our eye, with the pupil of the eye, it is as if we were touching the outlines of this object and follow it as we see these very outlines. We make tiny motions with our eye muscles to follow these outlines, as if we were touching the object. This function of moving our eye muscles Steiner ascribed not to our sense of sight, which he calls the sense of color, but to our sense of movement.

Illustration in Respect to Focused and Peripheral Vision

Regarding form drawing, when learning forms, be they letters or numerals, the outlines of maps, the basic form elements of animals or plants, or the forms of objects, patterns, even geometry, intense observation and imitation of these forms will enable children and adults to learn them. Usually the particular form needs to be grasped and repeated many times and in a variety of ways—on paper, walking on the floor, drawing into the air, in sand, on clay, and so forth. This imitation of the respective form does not require much intellectual understanding, but it does require a sense of movement and orientation.

Orientation is crucial for our capacity to imitate, because if we do not distinguish up or down, right from left, forward from back, then we cannot imitate. In other words, our capacity of knowing the dimensions of three-dimensional space is a necessity. Movement activity helps inscribe basic forms into memory. We have a different relationship with memories of our motions than with what is perceived intellectually, either through what is seen, heard, or thought. Repetitive actions help develop capacities. For instance, the repetitive drawing of the letter K while sounding its sound enables the young child to internalize its sound and remember its form. Eventually this learned form—together with all the other letter forms—enables one to read. Much of learning in the first years of school has to do with integrating our motion memories with our intellectual memories, which means that teachers need to continuously work at the integration of these two regions of our soul experience. This integration could also be called forming a relationship between head/nerves and limbs/blood.

Regarding technical and geometric drawing, clarity is essential regarding orientation in both the two-dimensional plane and three-dimensional space. In other words, students have to be taught how to fit their drawings into the grid of space. Of course, with maps this is also vital. We have here the necessity not only of fitting a specific pattern into the grid of space, but also of developing a sense for the relative position of its elements. This may be practiced by movement in actual three-dimensional space to awaken the sensitivity for relative position, before the whole-body motion is translated into a plane.[6]

One aspect of forms that needs to be understood with our intellect has to do with symbols. Letters, numerals, music notation and mathematical symbols have an extended meaning that needs to be learned and understood. I propose that when learning the meaning of these symbols we do so easiest when active in bodily motion, and so impress their meaning into our memory. I believe that learning these symbols is the equivalent of accessing the cosmic atmosphere of peripheral vision, wherein, like the starry constellations, the meaning of these symbols is always present, even if occasionally covered by clouds or flooded by the light of sun or moon. One could also describe knowing the meaning of symbols as a fundamental practice leading towards active imagination.

Interlude: Three-Dimensional Space and Its Perception by the Human Being

We have just explained the necessity for orientation, which implies knowledge of three-dimensional space. How do human beings develop knowledge and experience of the grid of space?[7] It begins in the first years of childhood when the child begins to stand upright, thereby conquering the vertical dimension. One could describe beginning to talk, that is, having interaction with his environment, as exploring the horizontal dimension, and finally moving in the medial plane when beginning to remember and think. This movement is much more internal and subtle, but is apparent in the relationship of the young child with sense impressions, particularly vision.

Thus the young child grows into a relationship to space. This is the basis for a good many achievements of learning later on in life. One should keep in mind how a disturbance in a young child's relationship to the three dimensions of space will hinder the school-age child in his or her learning to read and write.

It is clear that one cannot execute form drawings, technical drawings or geometrical drawings without observation and an understanding of how to fit objects into a spatial grid. All this is obviously connected to our focused vision. But what is the situation regarding imaginative and artistic illustrations?

When we allow our imagination to help us draw an imagined or historical event, it is our peripheral vision capacity that guides us. Remember the comment about the portion of the retina, the fovea, on which we project the objects of our focused vision: if the fovea were the size of the disk of sun or moon, and the rest of the sky is open, the peripheral portion of our vision would be comparable to the whole sky. Sensitivity for peripheral vision is also sensitivity for complementary colors. If a person has a particular propensity to see complementary colors easily, then, I believe, one might also assume that what lives in the atmosphere, either physically or spiritually, might have a strong influence on the capacity for forming imaginative visions. Imagination rules in the width of sky, the depths of the cosmos, that which is ever-changing, moving and apparently indistinct. We are entering the area of artistic imagination when we suppress our desire to focus precisely and allow a free play of possibilities into our consciousness. If the sun or the moon represents our focused consciousness, our full attention, then the sky of possibilities invites imagination into our souls. An example of this playfulness is when we can see animals or human figures in different cloud shapes. Imagination is all about possibility and not about something fixed to an external object.

Let us return here to the question of imitation and ask ourselves what imitation is actually good for. One answer is: technique—the learning of technique by example. Technique is learned through imitation. In the old painting workshops of the Renaissance masters, there were many apprentices who learned by imitation and were occasionally given the opportunity to fill in a painting that was incomplete. We shall discuss at this point several drawing and painting techniques and their essential aspects.

Watercolor painting:

In conventional watercolor painting, dry paper is used. A line of paint from a fairly solid palette is placed on the paper, lightened with water so that it flows into the desired direction and fills a desired area of the painting. This technique is very effective for clouds, trees, background landscape, and so forth. It has the advantage that portions of the painting may be *drawn with the brush*, thereby achieving sharp contours. The best way to learn this is to observe a master artist, then practice the adding of water and thinning down the bold color to achieve certain effects.

Watercolor painting in a Waldorf school is handled differently. The challenge set to students is to learn to control the water element. The paint is already mixed with water in pots, most likely just the primary colors in the younger grades and kindergarten. The paper is stretched and already wet. The challenge for the students is to learn how the combination of brushstroke, drying the brush and mixing colors on paper will render the desired effect.

Painting with oils and acrylics:

These paints needs to be mixed to the desired shade on a palette. It is more difficult to mix the colors on paper or canvas. In a Waldorf school students are not introduced to oil painting until the high school.

Form drawing:

Decorative patterns provide excellent practice for learning to write and then read. Steiner suggested that on the first school day in first grade students should be introduced to the forms of the straight and curved lines.

It is traditional in Waldorf schools that students first learn to walk in straight and curved lines, then draw them in the air, paint them and finally draw them on paper with crayon. There exists a multitude of patterns to supply these forms. Throughout the early grades much form drawing takes place, which activity benefits hand-eye coordination, as well as clarity of form to help develop clear handwriting. Form drawing practice strengthens the focusing capacity of the eyes. Pattern recognition strengthens the capacity to read. This will help later on when exact and accurate observations of objects or processes are required, for example, in the science studies.

Most beginning form drawing patterns are along a line and progress to the circular. The tools for beginning form drawings are usually crayons. Patterns may also be practiced with different colors. Later, probably in second or third grade, when writing with a pencil (usually color, eventually lead) is introduced, patterns are also drawn with pencil.

Technical drawing of a living entity:

Drawing animals, plants and minerals precisely is quite challenging for anyone not gifted in drawing. Students need to learn the major features of an animal, a plant and a mineral (crystal) by example and practice. To have students copy an animal form or a plant from nature is not a good idea at this point, because students do not yet know what they actually see and observe. Rather, it is a good idea to first discuss the prominent features, and then practice drawing these, and finally blend them into a drawing of the whole entity. For example, with mammals the line of the spine could be learned. The learning of this typical line—a big difference between an elephant and a bear, for instance—could be the foundation for learning this animal form. This could be practiced, repeatedly, on scrap paper, by using a linear stroke, say, from head to tail. The teacher's example on the board is essential here, because the typical features may be enhanced.[8] Very long strokes, lines that go along the spines of the respective animals should be used, with crayon or pencil, so that the eye learns to follow the contours of the spine. This technique, with the broad side of the pencil tip held sideways, could be called *following the form*.

Similarly with a plant, after discussion, the drawing may be practiced many times over before going out to find this particular plant in nature. It is quite important to discuss typical features and learn them by drawing before observing in actuality. In this suggested sequence the eye is trained to observe so that later on, in nature, the student can perceive details exactly.

Geometrical drawing:

In order to highlight different features of a geometrical drawing, color may be used. As careless coloring will smear the intended clarity of a geometrical construction, it is good to practice delicately *following the form* when using pencils to color. Again, when respecting the boundaries of a geometrical construction, the eye's focusing capacity is further schooled.

A similar process should be carried out when drawing maps. I personally do not suggest that maps should be copied from an actual printed map hanging in front of the classroom. I believe that maps should be learned using the same process used in learning to write. Maps should be walked on the floor and certain features discussed; students should practice for several days walking these maps in imitation of the teacher. Then they should draw from memory, so it is the memory of the activity of walking that is put down on paper, not what is displayed at the front of the classroom. After this the actual map could be placed in front of the students and compared with their drawings. In this way the process becomes a learning experience, and the forms of a map become internalized.

A final comment: Teachers should recognize that the learning of forms as described above means much practice, and therefore should be ready with much scrap paper. Also, the progression from broad crayon strokes to thin pencil lines should take place gradually. (There are many different opinions about when to introduce pencils. I believe that for the proper schooling of hand-eye coordination, stick crayons are effective through second grade, and the switch to colored pencils should take place in third grade.)

Imagination: Invitation by the Teacher

Imaginative illustrations depend on a teacher's verbal descriptions to spark or inspire a student's own inner visioning. While the details of a particular illustration, for instance as part of a main lesson book, may be discussed, the layout described and details mentioned, the overall illustration or painting depends on whether students develop an inner picture of the topic.

Human beings are very visually oriented. When a student is shown a picture, the tendency to imitate is very strong. Only when the capacity for inner pictures, when inner—that is, soul—envisioning is fostered, then will students be able to draw or paint what they see in their souls. Naturally, the fostering of inner vision goes hand in hand with the learning of techniques, so that the know-how of putting the inner vision on paper or canvas may be realized.

A particular technique that is used in Waldorf school illustrations has a relationship to peripheral vision. It is a technique that dissolves the solid contours of visual objects. A hatching stroke allows shading of colors as well as shadows and imitates the indistinct outlines of objects seen in a mist. This technique has several advantages when used for illustration, and it has distinct disadvantages when used for technical drawings. The advantage is that while a rhythmical laying down of a veil of strokes takes place, imagination is piqued, peripheral vision is invited, and the activity of the hand enables the mind's eye to construe possibilities for developing a scene. When using this technique, which needs much practice (usually begun in third grade), we are freeing the mind from focused vision and encouraging it to roam freely.

The encouragement and development of inner vision will take place via a teacher's verbal descriptions. Ordinary teaching methods (in regular or public schools) and relying on textbooks are not effective in helping students develop inner vision. Is the lack of verbal/direct descriptive instruction one reason that adults in recent decades lack imagination, obvious in many ways too numerous to elucidate?

One aspect of working with imagination in the Waldorf curriculum is manifest by having all students, from first grade through high school, make their own textbooks, or main lesson books, as they are called.

Interlude: Making Textbooks—a Student's Main Work

This is an aspect special to Waldorf education in which the free development of the students' mental and soul capacities are allowed, without being confined into conventional forms. Steiner mentioned making textbooks only indirectly, although it has been a custom from the beginning in the first Waldorf schools to do so. He did point to the following, when giving examples of students' practical work in making toys, handicrafts and handwork: "These practical activities have the character of free working while carrying this over into the artistic. The child should work out of its will, not out of prescribed and abstract ideas."[9] He stressed that it is essential for children to form and formulate their work according to life, to their natural and social environment, and not according to abstract ideas.

What does it mean to make one's own textbooks? Usually students are highly interested in their own work. There is an inherent sense in human beings to differentiate between imitating another or working creatively out of themselves. In the latter, human beings feel confirmed in their being. They prove themselves, they experience self worth. With every difficult task completed, one's self worth and self respect increases. Consequently, it is up to the teacher to find the right balance in assigning tasks—not so easy as to lower self worth but not so difficult that a child does not have the necessary skills to fulfill the task. In the end, the essence of the subject matter is made visible in a personal way and the students identify with the material.

Quicker and slower students often pose problems for teachers when tasks are either too easy or too difficult. It is possible, in the dynamics of a Waldorf classroom, to help slower students by working with them individually (usually at the board, with the teacher asking all others to go ahead with their assignments), and also giving additional special challenges for the quicker students. In this way, whether it is copying text from the board in the lower grades or finishing geometric constructions in the higher grades, it is possible to work with students of all capabilities.

What do the students learn when making their own textbooks? The will effort expended in writing and drawing, laying out and beautifying a page will strengthen the memory of what has been put down on paper. Clarity of thought, clarity of purpose, neatness of execution, and aesthetic design are all fostered. In other words, students may be proud of their achievements, and those not so gifted may learn to become more skillful.

Another aspect is the actual comprehension of the subject matter. When writing, technical drawings and artistic illustrations are combined to give a complete picture of a subject, of its essentials; a student is reminded of what he or she has learned and understood. The writing and drawing, illustrating and otherwise completing each chapter instills the appropriate sense of completion to the work. The beautification and aesthetic completion of each page make each book not only a record of what has been learned, but also provides pleasure to look at it. The soul element of feeling gets involved in both the conceptual element of understanding the subject matter and the will effort made to complete each page, and further serves to endow the book with emotional weight. Having their own textbooks in front of them, students are helped at the end of the year to review what has been learned and mastered and preview what remains to be learned and mastered in the future.

Steiner often depicted the main lesson block periods as giving both teacher and students the opportunity to enter deeply into a subject matter and spend several weeks in carrying through this main objective.

This gives the teacher time to expand on the main subject, dramatize it, make it interesting, relate it to poetry and song—in other words, expand on it artistically to give it depth, and so make it part of the students' life experience.

The Book of Life of every human being includes experiences, thoughts, habits—good or bad—capacities won or to be developed. Our memories consist very much of activities that we have enjoyed (whereas we often forget what gives us problems). Making one's own textbooks, with all the challenges, helps to add capacities and skills into a person's habits, whether the books deal with grammar, arithmetic, knowledge of the natural world, knowledge of human achievements in history or science, or an overview of the arts of humanity. One might say that making one's own textbook links each person, young or old, to the whole of human history and, further, expands personal knowledge in an orderly manner.

Although the younger students need to imitate good examples, they should be given the opportunity to develop the beautification of their pages on their own, even if they need to copy the text. Older students, from about third or fourth grade, should be encouraged to compose their own texts and copy them into their books after the teacher has checked them. From about sixth grade, students should be encouraged to write their own texts, possibly by dictation to begin with, and from seventh and eighth grades to design and execute their textbooks according to their own ideas. In high school students should be expected to be descriptive and precise in their writing as well as artistically competent in their presentation.

Illustration: the Blending of Technique and Imagination

Fulfilling Steiner's demand for artistic education comes about when from first grade on students use what they have learned about the techniques of drawing and painting in order to portray the essence, the kernel, of the main lesson. Younger students will need a great deal of guidance when making their books, art work, handicrafts, painting and drawing—in discussing appropriate colors, forms, and layout, according to the essence of the contents.

It is quite helpful to tell students, as they work on perfecting technique, that they are practicing. It is up to the teacher to make practice sessions interesting, in varying the tasks set before students. Here is an example an experienced Waldorf teacher shared with me many years ago. In learning about the details of maps, he suggested the students draw with blue pencil (crayon) precise strokes coming from the edge of the paper in a kind of frame of the map, leaving the actual form of it white. Then, on another day, he suggested they begin with red pencil (crayon) from the center of the space that the map has to eventually occupy, radiating out from the center, but stopping precisely at the edges of the map. In this way the actual form is learned, practiced, and becomes part of the student's memory of forms.

Beautiful writing is developed in a similar manner. It is good to highlight key words in a text as well as the title. That means that we discuss which color fits what the text is about, which color fits the content, so that there is a unity of expression. If a teacher works strongly with the temperaments, then it is not too difficult to guide students to choose the appropriate colors and forms or style of writing.

The whole class uses the same colors: active colors for the active characters, verbs, elements of a story, and so forth, and passive colors for the minor characters. If there is understanding of this concept in the class, the whole class should use these colors. Another aspect of choosing colors is to reinforce sentence structure and grammar. For instance, titles are one color, punctuation marks another, and important names still another. For the different parts of speech, again different colors are designated to them, by agreement under the teacher's guidance. (Remember, Waldorf education has nothing to do with free expression, but everything to do with suitable and appropriate forms and colors. It is the task of the teacher to discuss these forms and colors with the class and guide the feeling of students to be able to choose these.)

Imagination is fostered by conversation. The more a teacher is in the habit of discussing elements of the work with all students, the more their active imagination is stimulated to devote itself to the work. It is by listening to the teacher that the activity of inner picturing takes place. It is by painting word pictures that imaginative illustrations and the creation of significant pages arise in the students. Their active participation is the inner picture they create when listening. This is one of the aspects Steiner described about the importance of the will element in education. "This feeling for space, this feeling for form must grow in the child. It must grow right into the limbs. That kind of education has possibly a much stronger effect on the physical being of the child than active gymnastics… These considerations, going into all details of the above, bring about a living way of working. In this way education is preparation for life."[10]

Active listening is also fostered through conversation. Active listening may be a gift for life.

Final Comments

The intention of this article is to stimulate a teacher's thinking about the everyday activities in a Waldorf school. If we begin as teachers to understand the sense of sight, and all that it implies for the above considerations about illustration, imagination and imitation, then we will no doubt fulfill the task of educating towards the future of humanity.

"The sense of sight … is the sense where the sun of consciousness rises, and we reach full waking consciousness. The sun rises higher and higher. It rises to the sense of warmth, to the sense of hearing, and from there to the sense of speech, and then reaches its zenith."[11]

ENDNOTES

1. Paraphrased from Rudolf Steiner, *The Spiritual Ground of Education*, Lecture 7, New York: SteinerBooks, 2004.

2. Steiner, Rudolf. *Toward Imagination. Culture and the Individual*, Lecture on "The Twelve Human Senses," Hudson, NY: Anthroposophic Press, 1990.

3. Paraphrased from Rudolf Steiner, *The Spiritual Ground of Education*.

4. Op. cit., Steiner. *Toward Imagination. Culture and the Individual*.

5. Steiner, Rudolf. *Foundations of Human Experience*, Lecture 14, New York: Anthropsophic Press. 1996. See also Rudolf Steiner, *Practical Advice to Teachers*, Lecture 7, London: Rudolf Steiner Press, 1976.

6. See a description of such work in chapter 6 of the author's book *The Temperaments and the Arts*, Fair Oaks, CA: AWSNA Publications, 2003.

7. Steiner, Rudolf. *The Spiritual Guidance of the Individual and of Humanity*, Lecture 1, Hudson, NY: Anthroposophic Press, 1991.

8. Steiner even gave the example of a caricature to enhance the typical characteristics in Discussion 8, *Discussions with Teachers*, London: Rudolf Steiner Press, 1983.

9. Paraphrased from Rudolf Steiner, *Die geistig-seelischen Grundkraefte der Erziehungskunst*, [The Spiritual Ground of Education], Rudolf Steiner Verlag, GA 305, lecture of August 23, 1922.

10. Paraphrased from Rudolf Steiner, *The Spiritual Ground of Education*.

11. Op. cit., Steiner. *Toward Imagination. Culture and the Individual*.

Teachers in Tune with Parents
Striving Towards Healthy
Teacher-Parent Relationships

We speak of the astral body as long as we have in mind the birth of knowledge of an object that is present. What gives permanence to this object, however, we then call the soul.[1]

I would like to describe, from a teacher's perspective, how parents and teachers could work together. When parents and teachers have the same goals for children, then they will easily find a way to work together. However, if the goals are dissimilar, then the real work of cooperation begins. Working together is vital for the lives of children and their successful growing into the adult world.

First we shall consider what a human being is from the viewpoint of Spiritual Science. A human being manifests his essence, his eternal self, which is an eternal spiritual entity, clothed by a physical body. Attached to the physical body is the life configuration, ensuring the health and well-being of this physical body. The soul body, the astral body, attached to the eternal self, carries consciousness and mobility of limb within it, as well as many functions of mind and soul. Steiner described many of these functions and also their transformations over the course of historical development. Finally, there are some portions of the human entity that are not yet fully developed, but are in preparation. The spirit self is one of these, and the preparatory agent is a part of the human astral/soul body called the consciousness soul. In the child these aspects are in a process of developing and do not yet fulfill their roles as they will in the emergent adult.

Can we ascertain some probable goals that parents have, and, consequently, what kinds of pedagogical philosophy of schools and teachers they choose for their children? We shall mention a few of these goals briefly, even to the brink of irony, and so determine the different ways parents and teachers can choose to work together. As a way of introduction, we will characterize some of the soul attitudes that are found in both parents and teachers as they have developed in the course of humanity's historical development.

The Rational Soul—Leading to the Modern World View

> The "I" [eternal self] rises to a higher level of its essential nature when it directs its activity toward the aspects of this object-knowledge that it has made its own. Through this activity, the "I" detaches itself more and more from perceived objects in order to work within what it has made its own. The part of the soul where this happens can be called the intellectual soul or mind soul… Here the soul is totally given over to something external to it. Even what it takes possession of through memory has been received from outside.[2]

During the last four to five centuries much progress has been made in Western society largely regarding scientific knowledge, industrialism and monetary policy. Many individuals who subscribe to a scientific worldview will be proud of how far society has developed and will look down, possibly, on the more primitive existence of cultures other than their own, according to what they experience. If the goal of parents for their offspring is to give them a foundation for the fullest experience of the modern Western world, then they will obviously follow certain principles in selecting their children's schools. The parents themselves are most likely steeped in the basic principles of science; they are most likely what might be described by the term materialists; they might be keen for their children to participate as fully as possible in the political, financial and educational life that is upheld by the powers that be. It is important to these parents that their children absorb today's prevalent Western worldview respective of science, social goals and finances. This goal is best pursued in certain private schools, but is also the declared goal of public education. In the case of public education, the goal is obviously that good citizens, meaning compliant individuals, are fostered, who will become good taxpayers, obey the dictates of government and not exercise too much independent thinking. They are satisfied with the materialistic goals of amassing as much money as possible, subscribing to the prevalent scientific, that is, Darwinist worldview, follow the orders of materialistic doctors, and believe their governments. In the case of private schools, the goals are the same, but promoting leadership in these very same fields is also stressed.

In all cases, whether public or private schools, parents, once assured that their goals coincide with the stated goals of the respective schools, then may sit back, relax, and let the schools proceed to shape their students in this image. There exists a minimal amount of anxiety for parents as long as the grades their children earn will be sufficient to accomplish these stated goals. In this case, the assurances of the principal will often suffice that the school will promote the respective materialistic worldview of the parents for their children, and that the respective colleges and university entry levels will be achieved and acceptances will be forthcoming.

The Sentient Soul—Supporting a Traditional Worldview

We can immediately see how closely the human astral body is linked to the part of the soul that gives permanence to knowledge. These two things are united into a single element of our human makeup, so to speak, and, therefore, this union can also be called the astral body. If we want exact terms, we can also call the human astral body the soul body and the soul, to the extent that it is united with this soul body, the sentient soul.[3]

Many wonderful qualities of the human being exist within this sentient soul. While there is much consideration of everything pertaining to our senses and the experiences deriving from them, a feeling quality in respect to the world also describes much that lives in the sentient soul.

Many individuals have hopes and considerations for their children's schools somewhat different than those characterized by the rational soul. They are looking instead for a sense of security that an established school can provide, such as a religious affiliation, or other traditional institution, such as unions or the much vaunted family tradition of several generations. Many religious institutions provide a great sense of security—God and His representatives on earth, the priesthood, know best, after all.

It may be that parents seek to instill in their children a morality linked to a particular religious belief system. There are many religion-based schools in this country and also in nations worldwide. In most religious schools it is taken for granted that there will also be religious instruction alongside the subjects of general education, and that some subjects may be modified to fit that particular church's viewpoint. This fact separates out the true believers from other parents, but there are many who think that no matter what the particular religious beliefs are, their children will receive some moral values while attending religious schools.

Many parents feel that religious instruction helps instill morality. Is this so? One mistaken assumption is that morality is a matter of belief and not a matter of a general attitude to life. In order to help educate human beings towards being able to become moral, upright individuals as adults, it is not enough to believe, in this world of the twenty-first century, that religious education guarantees moral education. Such religious instruction often concerns only a specific group of human beings; in other words humanity in general is not honored by the commandments promoted by a particular religion. On the contrary, it is evident that in much of religious life today there is a divisive nature. It may be that specific commandments are used to drive a wedge between a particular group honoring a particular religion or sect and mankind as a whole.

Inhumane atrocities have been and are committed the world over in the name of religion. Apparently it is in the name of that particular religion, which is deemed so excellent by its adherents, that there exists a forceful drive to spread that religion and convert as many as possible to that particular belief system. Does this mean that the quantitative attitude of today's scientific outlook has influenced world religions in this respect? Missionary activity thus prevails, and is often carried further into actual physical violence. In this respect humanity has not matured very much. Therefore it seems that a religious education in this age does not guarantee that its adherents will respect fundamental human rights, and so show respect for all other human beings who might not follow their particular creed. Without going into details, which the news media supply in excess, it is clear that in many cases religion appears to cater to one-sided beliefs that actually encourage the committing of atrocities.

Nevertheless, especially in the Western world, many parents are convinced that a church-based education will encourage their children to follow a path of righteousness. Frequently Steiner mentioned that, as preparation for future human development, religion would become so individualized that one could say that each person, each individual, would end up following her or his own religion. Steiner in this context discussed religion as an individual's relationship to spiritual worlds. One mention of the challenges confronting humanity in our present epoch of evolution, which began in the fifteenth century, is in connection with the spiritual beings that are closest to human beings, the angels, and their work in human souls during sleep. One statement that could presumably cause us a good deal of soul searching is this:

> Through the pictures they [the angels] inculcate into the astral body, their aim is that in future time every human being shall see in each and all of his fellow-men a hidden divinity…To conceive man as a picture revealed from the spiritual world,…this is the impulse laid by the angels into the pictures. The bestowal to man of complete

freedom in the religious life—this underlies the impulses, at least, of the work of the angels.[4]

This influence is commencing in our present age, and it will take quite a while until it, as well as other impulses living in the souls of human beings, comes to fruition. In the meanwhile teachers and parents will have to deal with the impulses of freedom in other ways. There are other impulses laid into human hearts by the angels that may be felt by human beings in a variety of ways again.

Focusing again on the implications of morality in an age where apparently anything goes, a great deal depends on the individual and her or his picture of what is moral. For parents who choose religious schools in the hope that their children will have a firm foundation of morality for life, we should consider that a firm idea of what is appropriate behavior is really only possible when each individual human being makes this ideal a reality in her or his soul, and so subscribes to moral conduct. It is necessary that human beings become enabled to form a picture of what a human being actually is. Only then can morality permeate human interactions.

It is in the nature of many students to respect individual teachers as role models in a variety of ways. While a particular religious school, despite its advertising, may not actually help inculcate moral ideals in children, particular individual teachers, through their own conduct, may well achieve this.

Religious schools often promote a slavish devotion to one specific way of looking at life, at humanity, at the history of mankind. While this must be considered, it should not be confused with actual progress of human evolution.

The Consciousness Soul—Learning to Look into the Future with Deliberation

We can find a divine element in ourselves because our own primal being is taken from the divine. Thus, through this third part of the human soul, we acquire inner knowledge of ourselves, just as we acquire knowledge of the outer world through the astral body. This is why esoteric science can call this third soul element the consciousness soul.[5]

Steiner described the development of the soul attitude, or consciousness soul, as the advancement necessary for human development in our age. It involves human beings becoming aware of themselves as spiritual entities, as beings of both physical and spiritual worlds, as citizens of the cosmos, and as members of the whole of humanity.

> This, in a sense, is the call passing through humanity though dimly and inaudibly. But in the deep, underlying, subconscious longings of human beings lives the call, the wish to receive a content, substance, for the shadow nature of rational thinking. It does mean that today a more powerful force is needed in order to raise up what lies deep within the human being. We have to develop this stronger faculty, stronger in comparison to what was needed in earlier times. This is the task in the age of the development of the consciousness soul.[6]

While this consciousness soul has a somewhat hardened outer shell of the prevalent scientific attitude to life, in its inner core human beings are beginning to take a look at themselves and to learn strengthening of their soul qualities, so that they may become organs for spiritual perception. Indeed, it is crucial that individuals begin to develop these soul organs. If this does not happen in the course of the next few centuries, then perversions of physical life on earth will likely take place.

Purely through the Spiritual Soul, purely through their conscious thinking, men must reach the point of actually *perceiving* what the angels are doing to prepare the future of humanity.[7] Human beings actually need to begin considering themselves and other individuals as spiritual entities. They will need to respect everyone's religious freedom. Moreover, they will need to develop insights into the spiritual nature of the world. Unless these three attributes are fulfilled, perversions will shake up humanity, caused by adversarial forces that also play into human soul life.[8]

Many perversions of the social life, the scientific life, and the economic life will come about unless human beings begin in our age to develop their conscious life, their thinking capacities, and their moral capacities in the direction of developing the consciousness soul, which Steiner also called the Spiritual Soul, as it will develop eventually into the Spirit Self.

There are parents who, rather than spell out how much money their children should earn, how many university degrees they eventually might earn, or how much political standing they could achieve, are concerned with how they will act by serving humanity in today's society. Parents who genuinely wish for their children to do good are rare and often have a difficult time finding schools for their children with whose basic philosophy they are able to agree. Those parents who also want for their offspring to have insight into the realities of humanity and the world at large probably do not subscribe to a materialistic outlook on life. Many are inclined towards a spiritual way of looking at the world, but often in a non-sectarian context, because they realize that an overly religious orientation can actually cause partisanship.

In the writer's opinion, religious is not, repeat, not identical with spiritual. On the contrary, while in many people's lives religion is identifiable as a spiritual outlook, some individuals, including myself, are certain that spirituality means to envisage and encounter spiritual meanings and entities throughout the world, in nature and in human beings. Moreover, we subscribe to a conviction that in every human being lives an eternal entity that alternates a lifetime in a physical body with a purely spiritual existence.

These parents generally defy labeling; to label them Hippies, Followers of Alternative Mindsets, Cultural Creatives, Believers in Oriental Religions, and so forth, would not do them justice. Many are independently-thinking individualists; they are non-conformists who do not share the general public's outlook on life. It has been estimated that in the United States alone there are numerous people who follow a different drummer, whatever their particular interests may be.[9] In any event, the discovery of many individuals who do not buy into the prevalent worldview, no matter the particulars of their orientation, signals a shift in our Western culture. It may be that this shift inspires parents to search for schools that support their non-conformist opinions. Indeed, there has been a significant increase in home-schooling, which indicates to me that there are numerous parents who will not entrust the education of their children to the citizen factories of the public schools or to the materialistic positivists and secularists of much-vaunted private schools.

Many non-conformists take particular interest in environmental subjects. They find that in popular and materialistic culture there seems to be very little concern for the health of the whole earth. Of course any belief system, including this one, may also lead to extremes, such as eco-terrorism or the abject belief in global warming without checking the actual scientific data. The challenge in today's world is for human beings to be able to find a balanced viewpoint and resist the temptations of a one-sided point of view.

Many of these parents have been finding that Waldorf schools satisfy many of their beliefs. There are now some two hundred thirteen such schools and initiatives in North America. If parents of children that go to Waldorf schools are clear in their minds that they are looking for an education that acknowledges the spiritual nature of human beings and therefore treats children accordingly, then we are dealing with a significant membership of public life that is searching for a new culture. There can be little doubt that all those connected to Waldorf schools are exploring the possibilities to fulfill their longing for a new culture. In some instances parents confess that it is their children who have led them to the Waldorf school.

Before we actually consider some suggestions which might make it easier for Waldorf teachers to come to grips with parents' value systems, we must make a few cautionary comments and reiterate what has been described above. Such cautionary comments will, possibly, characterize some of the key differences of philosophical orientation in today's world. One of these directions, as I have attempted to characterize when discussing the rational soul orientation, has a great deal to do with the prevalent scientific view and the particular way that it colors the attitude of many individuals who are involved in business, science, education, medicine, the media and other occupations. These individuals believe in the determinism of Darwin's theory of evolution; they subscribe wholly, or at least partially, to the view that heredity and environment determine the development of individuals; they excuse lack of individual efforts to overcome societal disadvantages as the influence of the environment; and they clamor for effective ways of social engineering. They, in fact, deny that individuals may overcome their circumstances. They deny what has been touted in American history as the remarkable individualism that arose after the American Revolutionary War.

One might characterize some of the ideals leading to the American Revolution two hundred years ago that are now active in much of humanity on a global scale. But not everything that the West does in its foreign policy actually supports the cry for freedom heard around the world.

Another viewpoint, which I attempted to characterize when speaking of religious education and the sentient soul orientation, is the polar opposite view. By trusting established religious institutions to instill moral value systems in their offspring, parents rely on a belief system. In other words, they do not apply reasoning, nor a world view that is comprehensive, but narrow down their attitude that a particular belief system of the school and its teachers will do the right thing; that the force of religious belief represents the commandment of a higher authority; and that following this higher authority must be done no matter what. If, in fact, such individuals would apply their reasoning ability and their rational capacity to such belief systems, then they would have to recognize that following a belief system that commands a particular mode of behavior goes against the grain of human intellectual understanding and capacity. No matter what they proclaim, almost all churches, at the end of the twentieth century and the beginning of the twenty-first, show disrespect for human rationality.

While there is no doubt that many human beings simply know what is right or wrong in thought or action, it is also apparent that many individuals do not use their natural intelligence to discern this, but excuse their behavior by becoming followers of particular parties, churches, ideologies, and so forth.

Practical Advice

(1) It is vital for teachers to know and acknowledge the parents' goals for their children's education. If we are dealing with parents who subscribe entirely to the direction indicated concerning the rational soul—that is, with parents who have a materialistic bent and believe in the world according to Darwin—then we will understand that they will not have an easy time accepting many of the tenets of Waldorf education. However, they might understand that through Waldorf education their children will become considerably more rounded culturally, and so will be able to hold their own in terms of general culture with students in Europe and those from other parts of the world who have enjoyed a classical education.

(2) Regarding students whose parents believe in the moral values they expect will be instilled by a religious education, a different approach might be used by teachers in Waldorf schools. It might appeal to such parents that their children, in the course of their schooling, will receive an overview of all world religions, particularly in terms of their historical significance. Of course, a moral education per se would then not be bound up with a particular religious belief system, but would be expressed in general terms as a respect for humanity. While their particular church would provide particular religious instruction, a balanced worldview will be provided by the educational experience at school.

(3) Finally, for parents looking for something other than the prevalent

materialistic worldview or a religious education, it should be emphasized that their children will learn in a way that is more supportive for their subsequent adult life. They will learn to think independently and their intellectual achievements will be well founded. Many universities and colleges value students who have gone to Waldorf schools.

(4) In any event, it is imperative that teachers know a certain amount about the parents of the children they teach, such as their prevalent view of life, what their hopes and desires and plans are for their children, and so forth. This knowledge will help make communication between teacher and parent more fluid and successful. I well remember the comment one mother, a devoted Muslim, made to me when interviewing for the acceptance of her children into a Waldorf school, after I explained some of the subject matter of the grade school: "Good, then my children will have an idea of other faiths!"

Some Suggestions Specifically for Waldorf Teachers

(1) A vital principle of parent-teacher relationships has to do with participation. While teachers naturally regard themselves as professionals, and parents might be professionals in their own fields as well, many parents would like to participate, some to a lesser, and some to even a greater extent, in the school life of their children. How can this come about? Teachers might invite parents to sit in on classes, at least once a year, and so observe the students while working. This would require preparation for teachers. Students would have to be coached that the class will take place as usual, but their parents will sit in the back of the classroom and observe. The parents would be quiet and not interfere in any way. I have personally done this many times and have been told how parents appreciate such sit-in experiences.

(2) For parent evenings teachers might organize activities to present the subjects to the parents as if they were the children in class, and perhaps follow with adult explanation. Parents enjoy learning to use their colored

pencils for, for example, decoding grammar, or to do simple math problems notating them with color coding.

(3) Parents who ask to understand better the philosophical background of Waldorf education might be invited to a study group held by some teachers of the school. As some of Steiner's ideas are not easily absorbed, much preparation is needed and general explanations should be given before some of Steiner's basic pedagogical lectures are studied. It might be even advantageous that such a study be conducted not by teachers of a Waldorf school, but by members of anthroposophical groups, that is individuals well versed in Steiner's fundamental philosophy.

(4) Also, parents might be informed of Waldorf teacher training opportunities in the area, and they might participate out of interest, and so learn of the basic pedagogical principles as applied in Waldorf education, and, of course, entertain the option to become teachers, of which there is usually a shortage.

(5) Regular parent conferences are most valuable. In some schools special days during the year are set aside for this. It should not surprise teachers or parents that with some individual students their behavior is fundamentally different in school than at home. Regular conversation helps solve and bridge such challenges.

(6) Another helpful communication is the annual student reports given out at the end of each school year. Since Steiner's time there have been many changes in how these reports are handled by Waldorf schools.

In an education based upon knowledge of man, many needs become apparent which may have gone unnoticed in the more traditional forms of education...in this case, too, we felt the need of an innovation. For I must admit that I should find it extremely difficult to accept in a Waldorf school the usual form of school reports for the simple reason that I could never appreciate the difference between a "satisfactory" or "near satisfactory" mark, or between "fair" and "fairly good" marks, and so on. These marks are then converted into numbers, so that in Germany [of 1921] some reports show the various subjects arranged in one column, and on the opposite side there is a column of figures, such as 4½ , 3, 3–4, and so on. I have never been able to develop the necessary understanding for these somewhat occult relationships! And so we decided to find other ways of writing our school reports.

When our pupils go into their holidays at the end of the school year they, too, receive reports. But these contain a kind of mirror picture, a kind of biography of their progress during the year, written by their class teachers. And we have found again and again that our children accept these reports with inner approval. In them they can read what impression they have created during the year. They will feel that, although such a description has been written with sympathetic understanding, it will not tolerate any whitewashing of less positive aspects of their work. These reports, which are received with deep inner satisfaction, end with a verse, specially composed for each individual child.[10] This verse is a kind of guiding motif for the coming years. Our kind of reports, so I believe, have already proved themselves and will retain their value in the future, even though in some parts of Germany they have already been nicknamed as "Ersatz," as report substitute.[11]

It has become the habit in many schools, a little less than a hundred years after the founding of Waldorf education, to write reports directed to the parents, and not to the children. In some schools there are two reports written. I regret that also in some schools the reports are not sent out till after the beginning of the summer vacations, so that students do not receive from their teachers the review of the year as they should on the last day of school.

(7) While in this age, and particularly in the United States where the general public is so aware of grades and their importance for higher education, it is a good principle to also write reports for the parents specifically which translate some of what we would write for the students themselves into a format that parents would find helpful. In doing so, however, we

should make it plain to parents that the grades students receive, while possibly important for college acceptance, will perhaps be insignificant for the future adult life of their children. Most studies of students, their grades, and their college and university achievements do not extend into the students' adult lives to find out what they actually make of themselves in the course of a lifetime. This fact indicates the shortsightedness in today's attitudes, which do not take into account the long run. Thus, reports in the format of grades are for parents and university officials; reports for students should be framed on the essentially human content.

(8) Another aspect which parents often find confusing has to do with their children's artwork. It might be worthwhile for teachers to develop the capacity to analyze students' art to find typical formations pointing to a significant psychological feature, and then explain this to parents. In this way parents might train their perceptions to notice differences between their child's work and other children's. Also, it might be advantageous for teachers to have parents actually do artwork in the same format and process as the students are encouraged to do in class, for instance in a parent evening. *This might prevent parents from stating that all artwork of all students actually looks alike!*

(9) A further source of aggravation between parents and teachers has to do with behavior problems. While children will frequently overstep the bounds of acceptable behavior (this is of course a learning experience), continuous communications between teachers and parents may not be necessary if parents and teachers have worked out an acceptable code of behavior. Students, particularly in the older grades, should be informed of this code, and all teachers enforce it. It is possible that infractions of this code may have been caused by problems not immediately apparent. Certainly parents and teachers must communicate immediately if such an infraction arises. This requires that school policy is decided on how to handle severe behavior problems, and that all teachers, class teachers as well as subject teachers, openly support this policy. I certainly do not suggest that

parents contact teachers at all hours of day and night. A teacher who has to prepare for the next day's classes will not appreciate being contacted late at night, unless there is an emergency, and it would be best to tell parents what the nightly cut-off time is for such communications.

(10) In short, there are many problems that may arise in parent-teacher communication. However, some foresight on the part of teachers would go a long way to preventing crises of misunderstanding. Sometimes it is a good idea to have other teachers present to prevent misunderstanding when a particularly sensitive issue needs to be discussed.

(11) Parents resent it, and rightfully so, if teachers talk down to them. It is incumbent upon teachers to keep the level of communication as high as possible, and to show themselves to be as understanding as possible, while listening closely to parents. Parents know, often all too well, if there are internal problems in a school's faculty or administration, or whether the teachers of their children experience some difficulty or another. It would be futile to imagine that a faculty of teachers could build a wall around the school, and that the parents of their students would not know what goes on inside it!

(12) Many parents have asserted in many schools over the years that they feel it is their children who have led them to the Waldorf school. In some cases the children actually are fully active in this respect and say so to their parents, "This is my school." In other cases it is more hidden, and parents realize this fact only in retrospect.

Having the right relationships between the parents and the teachers has been important right from the beginning of the Waldorf school movement. While adjustments are needed for present-day conditions in all countries worldwide, the following remarks by Steiner elucidate some of the challenges:

We attach the greatest importance to our relationship with the parents of our Waldorf school children and in order to ensure complete harmony and agreement we arrange parent evenings fairly frequently, which are attended by parents of children living in the neighborhood. At these meetings the intentions, methods and the various arrangements of the school are discussed—naturally in a more or less general way—and, in so far as this is possible in such gatherings, the parents have the opportunity of expressing their wishes and these are given a sympathetic hearing. In short, by this means the mutual understanding between teachers and parents is not only of an abstract and intellectual nature, but a continuous human contact is brought about. We feel this contact to be very important, for we have nothing else to depend upon. To visit the parents in their home is necessary in order to foster in the parents a concern that nothing should occur which might damage the natural feeling a child must have for the authority of the teacher…for indeed most parents are jealous of their children's teachers. They feel as if the teachers want to take the child away from them; but as soon as this feeling is present there is an end to what can be achieved educationally with the child. Such things can, however, be put right if the teacher understands how to win the true support of the parents.[12]

ENDNOTES

1. Steiner, Rudolf. *An Outline of Esoteric Science*, Chapter 2, Great Barrington, MA: Anthroposophic Press, 1997.

2. Ibid.

3. Ibid, following the statement at the head of the essay.

4. Steiner, Rudolf. *The Work of the Angels in Man's Astral Body*, CW 184, London: Rudolf Steiner Press, 1972.

5. Op. cit., Steiner. *An Outline of Esoteric Science*.

6. Steiner, Rudolf. *Materialism and the Task of Anthroposophy*, Hudson, NY: Anthroposophic Press, 1987.

7. Op. cit., Steiner, *The Work of the Angels in Man's Astral Body*.

8. Ibid.

9. According to Paul Ray, the sociologist who called these individuals the Cultural Creatives, there are some fifty million in the United States alone and many more worldwide, particularly in Western Europe.

10. While the custom of writing verses has become accepted in many schools, for teachers not so literally gifted, stories and images might replace this custom.

11. Steiner, Rudolf. *Soul Economy and Waldorf Education*, Lecture 8, CW 303, Spring Valley, NY: Anthroposophic Press, 1986.

12. Steiner, Rudolf. *Human Values in Education*, Lecture 6, London Rudolf Steiner Press, 1971.

Moral Principles—Can They Be Taught?

Pedagogy will bear fruit especially when the virtues of courage and moderation will be seen in the right light. These virtues need to be considered individually by educating children in such a way that they will retreat gradually from creating sorrows for themselves.[1]

One might have to delve deeply into aspects of what a human being actually is to understand the question in the title of this paper. Spiritual beings have given many gifts to humanity in past ages of human development. These gifts may possibly be misused, for that is the privilege of human freedom. However, these gifts may also be nurtured, and in this sense, affirm and show how both parents and teachers may support the natural development of moral principles in children and adolescents.

Steiner speaks several times of virtues related to morality, virtues that were already recognized in antiquity, for instance by Plato.[2] Steiner describes these virtues and brings them into connection with human physiology, for the human constitution of the physical body itself has been endowed with the potential of serving human beings towards developing morality. One aspect of helping parents and teachers help children develop a moral outlook is to understand how the human constitution is related to these virtues, because the physical body is in its very essence supportive of the essentially human element, which by its very nature is an element of morality.

Human Freedom

Whenever we focus attention on morality, we also need to consider human freedom. Human freedom needs to be defined more closely for our purpose. If we are honest with ourselves, it becomes quite obvious that we are free only in certain aspects of our existence, but that in some others we are either only partially free or entirely bound and lack any freedom at all.

How do we, in the course of everyday life, experience freedom? Is it the ability to act as we please? If we think that, then we probably would fall foul of our fellows. What is it that confines human beings and so limits the appearance of freedom? Social conventions, habits, personal convictions, the obligations and requirements of authority and our superiors, and other demands of personal and professional life. If we are honest with ourselves, the only characteristic of our life that allows us complete freedom is within our mind. Within our mind we are free to shape ideas, convictions, opinions and interpretations of what we notice and experience without coercion from others. We are quite capable of coercing ourselves, however, through our own convictions, so it is not entirely simple and easy to be completely free from the influence of others, nor of our own foibles. As a matter of fact it takes a certain amount of effort to come to a place of complete impartiality, where we know ourselves to be free from the influence of our own and others' opinions and prejudices.[3]

Whether we are completely impartial in our minds, free from the influence of ourselves—as in a favorite idea—or of other authority, it is most likely that we come to experience freedom only in our thinking and mental processes.

Social Conventions and the Human Psyche

Not so in respect to other areas of life: We find ourselves compelled quite frequently by our daily habits—eating, drinking, sleeping, dressing, talking to others—in short, by everything that requires interaction with other human beings. The social conventions give us space within which we are free to organize our lives as we will. However, whenever we take more than our allotted space or time, we immediately come up against societal restrictions. Some of these restrictions are formal—laws; some are more informal—customs and social habits.

Personal space in regards to social conventions is not usually clearly defined. There appears to be a natural space around each human individual that identifies her or his personal space, which varies from culture to culture. Such personal space extends to one's possessions: in childhood, to one's toys; later on, to one's property, which may be real estate or simply one's workspace, one's desk and its accoutrements. Personal space also seems to have a lot to do with personal dignity. We feel threatened or imperiled if this personal space is breached.

An interesting example of such personal space, however not relevant to our present discussion, with regards to work and labor is the following: An eminent economist describes how capitalism thrives in the Western world but languishes elsewhere because the instrumentation of proving personal property is not sufficiently established; consequently people in a Third World country, for instance, cannot secure loans for the businesses they wish to create.[4]

The personal space around each human being needs to be recognized and affirmed by society at large, acknowledged and honored, and so her or his personal possessions. Capitalism has a great deal to do with matters concerning the human head (e.g., the Latin root of the word). The human head conveys a relationship to property, to selfhood, to a person's immortal being, and also to a person's ideas and plans of action. Property rights include intellectual property. We experience what lives in our heads as ideas and plans specifically our own, and, unless we share it with others, we imagine that they would not know our secret ideas.

Actually what is happening is quite different. We are placed into a cosmic world through our ideas to participate with living human beings, but also with others who have returned to the spiritual world. Ideas, intentions, plans, and so forth, may come to us or appear "out of the blue," and we actually do not know their point of origin. Because we are under the delusion that our head is a closed-off space, and that we control it entirely, we usually pay no attention to the origin of ideas. In this regard we already need to reconsider the realm of life, where ideas, plans for action, and our thoughts in general are alive and interact with the ideas of others, with our culture in general. This is the sphere of the world which Steiner calls the sphere of the ether, the sphere of the life forces that underlie all living beings, whether plant, animal or human. This sphere of the life forces is the real home of all thoughts and ideas. The human body is in contact with this sphere via the human head, where the eternal self (the ego) and also the forces of the astral body (our consciousness and movement organization) are freely interacting with cosmic forces, namely the forces of the ether world. This interaction is going on below the level of our day-time consciousness. This point of view is in contradiction to the belief in present-day mainstream science that everything that goes on in our own head—the interplay of ideas and plans for action—exists solely in our physical brain and nervous system.

The First Platonic Virtue: Wisdom

But it is through the head that morality pours in when it encounters the ego forces in the blood.[5]

Steiner calls this world of ideas, that we assume is known to humans alone, the world of the life forces, the ether, and calls the virtue by which we may become aware of this world, the virtue of wisdom. Steiner discusses four virtues that together make up our morality. Wisdom is one, and is particularly related to the human ego, the eternal essence, and to the human head.[6] When ego forces pour through a person's blood, they energize this person, and so we may use wisdom in our actions deliberately. Coursing within us, uniting the whole physical body with our mind and soul, our blood leads us into will activity. If we are to act consciously, and with the right respect towards others, then we must consider all possible consequences of our actions towards individuals, towards society, and towards the world —this requires wisdom, foresight and forethought.

The relationship between wisdom and the human ego is astonishing. By learning throughout life, by learning from one's mistakes, it is possible to increase one's life's wisdom. According to Steiner, this capacity of learning from one's life extends to learning from one's past incarnations. However, this usually does not happen by conscious design, as, at the present time, there are relatively few individuals who have a sense of their past incarnations. We experience ourselves as being most conscious in our head; our sense impressions stir us up; they awaken us; they call upon us to react to them; they stimulate our consciousness—not always in a positive way, as, for instance, when we need to resist advertising. Other sense impressions tend to drive us with extraordinary power towards actions which we would not do if we had been able to keep a cool head. Thus the virtue of wisdom associated with our head, with our intelligence, means we reflect before we act.

How might we encourage children and adolescents to develop this virtue? The end result would be a recognition that human beings learn throughout life, that we can learn to change or adjust our actions, to recognize past erroneous behavior, and so resolve to not only learn from it but also not repeat it. This is a point not easily brought home to children and adolescents; they quite naturally resent having to listen to moralizing speeches and demands. How then can we accomplish the task?

We must provide examples by action, and not by talking about our ideas in a rational manner. There are historical examples of individuals who have acted out of moral principles, for instance Gandhi on the Salt March. We can tell stories, particularly to the younger children, in which the consequences of unconscious, irreverent, spiteful or malevolent actions are depicted pictorially. History is rife with numerous examples for older students.

Another way to gradually increase thoughtfulness might be to review from time to time the results of actions, thoughts and ideas. We can mention from time to time what will be learned in the future, several years, or even several days hence. A time perspective is thus encouraged and is entirely appropriate for an area concerning activities of knowledge, wisdom and life events. Of course for teachers there comes the time of year for writing reports; this is an excellent opportunity for a review of past achievements and a preview of future potential. Parents could make the opportunity at birthdays or some other occasions, where one might discuss future as well as past events.

The whole sphere of wisdom, while related to the sphere of the human head where ideas and thoughts live in the cosmic ether world, is also related to time itself, to the changing rhythms of time, to forgetting and remembering, and so to memory as such.

The Second Platonic Virtue: Courage

Consider the virtue of fortitude or courage. On the one hand, human nature may swing toward recklessness, that is, toward unrestrained activity in the world with full exertion of all one's forces. That is on the one side; on the other side there is cowardice. The human being can swing, as it were, to either side. For what is evil? Evil is what originates when we either lose out to the world or the world is lost to us. The "good" consists in avoiding both of these.[7]

It is quite a challenge for human beings to use the potential for a courageous action in such a way that no harm befall other human beings. We can see instances of this challenge every day. Present-day life has changed in remarkable ways from even two hundred years ago. In our present-day society, at least in the Western world, there is not much need to have physical courage, except in response to natural disasters or conditions of war. Can this be the reason that so many young human beings engage in reckless behavior, because society at large does not require courage in more physical and conventional ways? Courage might often be transformed from a bodily expression to a purely mental display. A public show of courage, as for instance with a person who is a whistleblower, has become quite common. Daring displays, particularly from younger people, take many forms, from clothes to behavior. Therefore, what kind of courage might be expected or appropriate in today's world? In his novel *1984*, written quite some time ago, George Orwell envisaged what might become of a world given over to mental slavery. I believe his descriptions, as well as the descriptions in the science fiction classic, *Fahrenheit 451* by Ray Bradbury, are really solicitations for all human beings to develop mental courage.

What is mental courage? One aspect of courage has to do with maintaining a balanced, middle position in this present world, rather than allow extremes. Mental courage means to recognize a balanced and therefore also impartial stance. It takes mental courage for a respective individual to carry out her or his judgment, fully cognizant of consequences.

Courage has since olden times, and rightfully so, been associated with the human heart. Steiner makes this same connection and elucidates it further by connecting the seat of courage in the human heart with an individual's astral body, her or his purely spiritual organization of movement and consciousness activities.

Whenever strength of heart—strength of mind, industriousness of the soul—streams down out of the moral sphere, it streams into the area of the chest, which encloses the heart. We can say, when morality radiates down [from the head], it is here, in the area of the chest and heart, where it particularly takes hold of the astral.[8]

What might this mean? Would mental courage also have its seat in the heart? In recent years the idea of "heart thinking" has been spoken about by a number of anthroposophists. Such heart thinking calls on practices other than intellectual thinking. Whenever we use heart thinking—and it is not infrequently that we do so—we are secure in ourselves, we feel ourselves in balance in our point of view, so that the world does not overwhelm us, nor do we give in to the world. I believe that this is one aspect of heart thinking, and one aspect of not giving in to evil temptations.[9]

We are now dealing with quite other capacities in human beings than the conscious cultivation of wisdom. We are now dealing with an area of human consciousness where we are, most of the time, neither aware nor fully awake, where we do need to make judgment calls, where we do need to take responsibility on a personal level, and where we need to follow a feeling of doing the right thing. A sphere where there exists a good deal of uncertainty, because we are compelled to make steps forward into the unknown. Courageous steps into the unknown are the challenge for present-day humanity. Whenever we follow the heart in this balanced way, we are certainly exercising a moral right of action.

One way we might view the seat of courage in the heart is in interaction with our head. What is the relation of wisdom to courage? What is it that holds us back from reckless actions, from going head over heels (actually the reverse is true) into an activity that we will eventually regret and wish that we had thought through before acting? It is apparent that our head and our heart need to work together. Our eternal self, our ego, has the task to control the astral body, the seat of movement and consciousness. In other words, we are challenged to become ever more vigilant and conscious of how we act.

Some decades ago a very curious event took place: At the beginning of the Kennedy Administration, a group of professionals, members of diverse disciplines, assembled, with the purpose and mission to determine whether there exist legitimate alternatives to war. When looking at the challenges of this period, we need to realize that this was the time of the Cold War, that the Soviet Union and Communist China were great powers, a significant challenge to the Western world. What could possibly replace a physical expression of courage? What could be the reality of peace?

The word *peace,* as we have used it in the following pages, describes a permanent, or quasi-permanent, condition entirely free from the national exercise, or contemplation, of any form of the organized social violence, or threat of violence, generally known as war.[10]

At the time the fifteen members assembled, meeting over about two-and-a-half years, could not come up with anything viable that would, in an economic, political, sociological, ecological and cultural setting replace what war has meant for human societies since antiquity, despite making several suggestions, including an expanded space program. It was recognized that human beings, for their mental health and stability, needed to be able to face danger. The overcoming of danger, physical or mental, would sharpen a person's physical and mental capacities and, in so doing, strengthen her or his immortal self. Relatively few occasions exist in our programmed world to exercise courage in the face of danger. No wonder that there exists a vast literature wherein many individuals may experience vicariously such elements of danger.

The need for human beings to express courage is a very deep-seated need. Why does it need to be expressed physically? What is the intention of peace activists in the present, and can their intentions actually be realized? Without the possibility of human beings showing some kind of physical, bodily expression of courage, a condition of peace anywhere in the world seems very unlikely. Do other means exist of expressing physical courage other than bravery in times of danger? Might it be appropriate to say, as human development has progressed since the beginning of the twentieth century, that now is the time where mental courage, not only physical courage, must be learned? Think of the atrocities that were perpetrated upon millions of human beings in this last century. Not only physical courage, but also mental courage was needed in order to defend one's own humanity from mental and physical slavery, and many human beings did exercise such mental courage.

We have seen an escalation of violence in society in recent decades, a time during which war has been a direct concern for Western countries. Has this become the equivalent of war? Does gang warfare replace organized military hostilities? Not easily answered, these are questions for society, for the well being of nations. Can conflict be fought and determined by other than physical means?

What is the quest for boldness, for courage, that lives naturally in every human being, which every human being strives to fulfill in order to have self respect? Is there a deep-seated need for human beings to face danger, to face the unknown and be recognized for this bravery by their fellow men? Is there another region of the human soul where courage is required? Can danger and the unknown be found in other locations, other places than the physical world? Two areas that many human beings shy away from are (1) self development and (2) consciously and deliberately following disciplines towards expanding their consciousness in ways not found in the physical world. Quite other dangers lurk there. And these dangers must be faced with courage—mental courage.

I am reminded here of some features described by Steiner about the actual tasks and mission of the present-day fifth Post-Atlantean epoch. By the beginning of the next epoch, the soul capacities of the Consciousness Soul need to be transformed into the forces of the Spirit Self. What might this mean? Steiner explains that, beginning in our age, quite new conditions have arisen for human beings that require work in the inner world of the soul.

Plato's Third Virtue: Moderation

The third virtue is connected with even less complete organs of the human body [than the heart or the brain]; it will gain its actual form later in human development and is present today only in potentiality. It is the virtue of moderation. It could also be called sun-filled-ness. Of course one can be immoderate in many ways. But whenever we take our desires in hand, limit our bodily responses to external stimuli, we create order in the forces that we shall not deliver to Lucifer in our next incarnation. We shall however deliver these forces that live in our digestive system and metabolism if we indulge in any form of passionate delirium.[11]

This virtue of moderation is very difficult to achieve in today's world, in which our desire nature is continually assaulted with demands to lose ourselves through our passions. I shall not here enumerate all the possible temptations to be immoderate, but shall leave this to the reader's imagination.

Steiner mentions that the virtue of courage is also threatened by the Luciferic forces. Both courage and moderation must become controlled by the human ego, by the power of the individual. And Steiner points out how essential it is, if our present stage of human evolution is going to successfully move into the future, that regarding pedagogy the virtues of courage and moderation must be stimulated and practiced.

Human desires are aroused in the abdomen, and the temperate person is the one who is able to rule over his desires by thinking about them, feeling his way into them and consciously experiencing them. It is no virtue to live a life that simply chases after desires…Temperance first arises when the desires are made as conscious as it is possible for them to be made. This happens in the ether body.[12]

Consequently when exercising control over any passionate reactions we enable the sun-filled area of our human constitution to emerge. It might be relevant here to note that the German word for "diaphragm" in our abdomen is *Sonnengeflecht*, "sun-network."

In ancient times the denying of sensory pleasures was an essential means to achieve spiritual enlightenment. In medieval times the elimination or denial of one's desire nature was equated with religious sainthood. What was not considered in the past was that there can be progress in spiritual development only if the soul no longer feels the urge for physical satisfaction of that person's desires. Today we might smile at the medieval monks or nuns who believed they could whip themselves into sainthood. Today we must go about achieving moderation of all things in life in a different way.

One aspect of the virtue of moderation is recognizing the temporary nature of everything in the physical world. What is permanent is the essence of the individuality, our own spiritual being. The challenge of moderation or temperance is to look at ourselves and at other human beings as spiritual beings. Steiner says that the virtue of moderation is the virtue to be especially practiced and developed in our present age, the age of the Consciousness Soul:

> Now we still have to consider what may be called the virtue of the consciousness-soul: temperance or self-discipline. In the fourth post-Atlantean cultural epoch these virtues were still instinctive. Plato and Aristotle spoke of them as the chief virtues of the consciousness soul, inasmuch as they considered them to be the mean of what exists in the consciousness-soul. The consciousness soul arises when the human being becomes conscious of the outer world by means of the physical body. The body that has evolved to serve the consciousness soul can be crushed by the world, or the human being can come to lose contact with the world. Temperance is the virtue that enables the human being to avoid both of these extremes. Temperance is neither asceticism nor self-indulgence, but the proper mean between the two. This is the virtue of the consciousness soul.[13]

Now we can understand why Steiner says that today it is especially important that both the virtues of courage and moderation should be brought to children as part of their education. Courage must be transformed from physical courage to mental courage. Moderation indicates a shift from simply accepting the validity of the physical, sense world by also empowering one's view of the validity of spiritual forces in the sense world, together with the validity of spiritual beings acting on, and on behalf of, human beings.

Another aspect of the virtue of moderation has to do with its connection to time. Indeed, temperance has its root in the Latin word for "time." The timing of one's actions may lead to self-indulgence, to asceticism, or to moderation. As a conscious individual one ought to consider the best timing for one's planned actions, and in the larger picture, the overall purpose of one's life. It is particularly vital in this our age of the consciousness soul to become sensitive to the timing of one's actions before birth and after death, that we consider the relationship of our eternal self to aspects of time. When considering time we may find the way towards a connection to spiritual worlds. Particularly when we are involved fully in matters of physical reality the timing of events becomes crucial. One example of the present day is the lack of foresight in the administration of many financial institutions, which frequently choose making profits in the moment over building lasting products or productivity. In this sense the virtue of moderation, as a virtue linked to an individual's ether body, has a great deal to do with how an individual conducts her or his life.

How can we help today's children and adolescents challenge themselves to mental/spiritual courage and also learn moderation? It is certainly not easy because the temptations to deny or avoid both are very great indeed. We shall consider this later.

Plato's Fourth Virtue: Justice

Plato's word *justice* refers to the ability to give our lives direction, the ability to know ourselves, to orientate ourselves in life. Morality begins on Earth; but Earth also makes the completion of a higher order, one that was already beginning on Saturn. So we have another stream, another order, that flows from Saturn to Earth, and we will now call that the stream of justice—justice in the sense that was explained earlier. As you know the senses had their beginnings on Saturn. These senses have the tendency to scatter a human being in all directions. You know that we distinguish twelve senses. The development of the twelve senses through Sun, Moon and Earth [evolutionary stages] leads mankind to justice, to a rightness and uprightness that also includes moral justice and moral uprightness once it has been taken hold of by the moral nature of the Earth. Moral justice first makes its appearance on Earth. And justice works inwardly to counter the peripheral tendency of the senses; the sphere, or stream, of justice works toward the center.[14]

Steiner asserts that the moral qualities have been connected to the essence of humanity since the very first stage of the cosmic evolution of earthly existence. The virtue of justice in this sense is related to the human physical capacity to stand upright. This is a gift of the spiritual world that enables the human being after birth to gain uprightness and language.[15] Soon after birth a child is able to orient her- or himself towards the stars (uprightness) and towards other human beings (language). The senses play a pivotal role in this capacity. Another capacity that awakens in young children soon after that time is memory, and so the capacity to experience continuity of being and with it the ability to say "I" to oneself. Memory is directed towards one's inner experience, not towards something external, although one's experiences of the external world result in memories. And so the third direction that is taken by the sense of justice is toward one's memories, towards one's center, towards oneself. In other words, the whole physical human being is concerned with justice, and particularly so in early childhood.

Whoever would exercise this virtue of justice would place every thing, every being on its right and correct location; she or he would enter into others, would leave her or his own self. This means to live within all-encompassing justice. We originate from the cosmos; heavenly forces permeated us in earlier incarnations. When practicing justice we unfold cosmic forces, but spiritually. Justice represents the measure of how humanity is related to the divine. Injustice practically becomes loss of divinity; it shows loss of the divine.[16]

Steiner relates the virtue of justice to the whole human being. The whole body is involved as the newborn child penetrates her or his body and accomplishes uprightness, and soon thereafter enters the world of language, and finally learns to direct her- or himself towards the inner being by re-living memories.

We may now summarize the four virtues in connection to our bodily existence and our spiritual constitution:

Virtue	Part of Human Body	Part of Human Constitution
Wisdom	The human head	The Eternal Self or Ego
Courage	The human heart	The Human Astral Body
Moderation	The human abdomen	The Human Ether Body
Justice	The whole human body	The Physical Body

In other words, the whole human being is constitutionally predisposed towards morality. Whenever we nurture any of the above *virtues*, we foster morality in the growing child and adolescent.

The Adversaries of Human Morality

Two virtues enlighten previous incarnations: Wisdom and Justice.
Courage and Moderation however enlighten future incarnations.[17]

There is another aspect of these four virtues we should consider: the spiritual powers that are adversaries of human development in the way that the great gods, the very highly developed spiritual beings who provide the guidance for humanity, have envisioned. These adversaries of humanity have been allowed, so to speak, to wreak havoc and confusion among human beings in order that each person find her or his proper relationship to her or his essential and spiritual self, as well as to spiritual worlds. The working of these adversaries, on the other hand, tends to obliterate, disguise or veil the real spiritual connections between human beings and their tasks in the world at large.

Lucifer and Ahriman have great interest in enticing human beings away from the path of development which the spiritual beings have designed for humanity. The virtues of courage and moderation may fall prey to the temptations of Lucifer. How? Both these virtues prepare in the present life the physical body of a future life. If a future life's body is compromised, then this future life will no longer be of consequence for the development of the whole of humanity.

A great deal of meaning has to do with the timing of one's actions, as mentioned above.

> When we refuse to exercise wisdom and justice, we may easily fall prey to the temptations of Ahriman, and whatever we need for the development of our future physical body would fall prey to Lucifer whenever we refuse to act with courage or moderation.
>
> Wisdom and courage are impossible to carry out unless we become selfless. Only the person who is selfish becomes unjust. Through both wisdom and justice we reach out beyond our own self towards the whole of humanity...Egotism becomes naturally selfless whenever we expand it over the whole of life, when we light up the horizon of life in terms of justice.[18]

The adversaries tempt us to do either too much in terms of selfishness, or too little. The challenge of these virtues, together with everything we do in life, yet again is living a life in balance, a balance of neither too much nor too little, a balance of neither too early nor too late, a balance of neither too materialistic nor too spiritual.

While we are incarnated in a physical body, surrounded by the physical world of nature as well as the machinery and technology invented by human minds, we should not lose ourselves to the other extreme by denying the physical world, but recognize it as an expression of spiritual forces. As the human being is also a spiritual being, her or his creations in terms of technology must also be recognized as spiritual creations, but of a lower level than the creation of nature by sublime spiritual beings, or the creation of the human body itself.

Regarding the temptations of Ahriman to the virtues of wisdom and justice, a very peculiar fact plays a part: Ahriman is a spiritual being, but supports materialism which denies any spirituality. How can this be? By denying that the human being had an existence in spiritual worlds prior to birth, and in particular had formed her or his body with the help of spiritual beings in preparation for a physical incarnation, the spiritual essence of a human being comes into doubt. Wisdom has relevance only if we accept the spiritual nature of human beings. Justice is negated whenever the spiritual nature of human beings is doubted. Both are confirmed by a human being's knowledge of spiritual worlds, by knowledge of pre-existence in spiritual worlds, and by knowledge of going back to a purely spiritual existence after death. In other words, if a human being acknowledges that a life span in a physical body is but an interlude in a purely spiritual existence, then the virtues of wisdom and justice will support this spiritual existence. Meanwhile, Ahriman would have humanity accept that a one-time physical existence is everything.

The divine powers have allowed Lucifer and Ahriman to place obstacles to understanding in man's path so that through individual efforts each person may break through to understanding of her or his relationship to spiritual worlds. We might be reminded here of the relationship of the virtue of courage in our own epoch, when mental courage, facing danger, is crucial. Where might mental courage be more appropriate than when recognizing Ahriman and Lucifer and their obstacles?

Actions of the Adversaries to Humanity in Respect to Moral Qualities

We touch on a point that is far removed from what is prevalent to day, namely, what Plato still called the ideal of wisdom. Since he used a word that was commonplace at a time wisdom still lived instinctively within people, it will be good to replace it with a different word. Because we have become more individualized and have distanced ourselves from the divine, it will be good if we replace it with the word *truthfulness*.[19]

It is apparent how much truthfulness is needed in the world today and how vital truthfulness is in terms of education. There exist so many opportunities for lack of it: what the media proclaim, what is told students in school, what human beings learn in their relationships to each other, let alone in politics. The manipulation of truth is very common. Education towards truthfulness as a transformation of wisdom would be of tremendous benefit to humanity in today's world.

Further, we should look at the possibility of the transformation of justice. Both wisdom and justice, according to Steiner, are threatened by the onslaughts of Ahriman on human souls. Justice is based on a human being's whole body, on the gifts that spiritual beings laid down into his capacity to orient him- or herself towards the good. Human beings may find this orientation out of themselves, out of their conscience. For what actually is conscience? Is it a nudge by our soul to reconsider our actions? Is it a nudge by our soul to think of the consequences of our actions? It appears as something placed deeply inside our whole humanity to help us realize what we are actually doing. Ahriman wants us to deny what the spiritual beings have laid into our bodies, and so act in the world without conscience, nor care of consequences. It is our conscience that holds us back and reminds us of our humanity. May we never lose it.

Similarly the concept of courage must be transformed to become meaningful in today's world. The change that Steiner advocates may at first be misinterpreted:

> Genuine love is brought about by the transformation of courage and fortitude. This genuine love, however, must be guided by the other virtue, by genuine interest in the being toward whom we direct our love… so also in human nature must the virtue of love be harmoniously guided by interest. The interest that brings us into relation with the outer world in the right way must lead and guide us when we turn our love to the outer world.[20]

This indicates a direct connection between courage and education. It is the task of teachers to stimulate the interest of their students. When students are not stimulated, they experience their schooling as boring, they have problems in going out of themselves into the world. But this very going out of oneself is crucial towards developing interest and love for the world at large. Students need to widen their hearts, embracing the world at large, learning about its many fascinating phenomena, and so develop a love for this world. Many teachers are able to stimulate the students in their care towards developing this interest in the world of phenomena.

One aspect of developing interest has to do with a questioning mind. Teachers who suppress the asking of questions stifle, even kill, interest in the world. Teachers who invite questions support the development of interest and with it the transformation of courage—the capacity to confront the unknown—into interest and love. What would be the transformation of moderation apropos to our present time?

> If people used all of their forces only to satisfy themselves, they would shut themselves off from the world; the world would lose them. On the other hand, people who deny themselves everything increasingly weaken themselves and are eventually crushed by the external world process. People who overtax the forces allotted to the human being are taken up by the world process and lose themselves in the world. The body that has evolved to serve the consciousness-soul can be crushed by the world, or the human being can come to lose contact with the world. Temperance is the virtue that enables the human being to avoid both of these extremes.[21]

It becomes clear that all adults around children and adolescents have the task, the challenge, to exercise moderation in daily life, not an easy task. As both parents and teachers know, rationalization will probably get one nowhere. It might be necessary for each adult dealing with a child or adolescent to find ingenious ways, imaginative pictures to moderate the too much or too little of the child's passions.

With regard to this virtue, we have not yet progressed beyond the instinctive standpoint. With a little reflection you can see that, on the whole, people are very much given to sampling the two extremes; they tend to swing back and forth between them. In this area people are still in a very instinctive condition, and we must say it is a kind of divine legacy that people still have an instinctive feeling to not do too much in the one direction nor in the other.[22]

Steiner points toward a main virtue in future human development: moderation will be of great importance in the next cultural epoch, the sixth post-Atlantean epoch.[23] Moderation as a virtue is essential not only for each individual human being's successful living, but also in one's dealings with others. For instance, when human beings are conscious, aware and willing to put themselves into another's shoes, then a tremendous turnaround of social values is likely to occur. Indeed, how much longer can the structures of Western society continue to maintain the world safe for multi-national corporations? How much longer should one protect the haves from the have-nots? The implications of moderation, of temperance, for responsibility in terms of society at large are looming conspicuously over our present world.

If enough young people are educated towards transformation of courage into interest and love and transformation of moderation into social responsibility, into conscience, then we may help strengthen the resistance to Ahrimanic and Luciferic temptations which would leave human beings mired in selfishness for their own goals, without regard for the higher interests of human development.

Again, one means to encourage children and adolescents to practice courage and moderation is to tell, as vividly as possible, tales of historical and imaginative events of men and women who have practiced these two virtues. Anticipation and timing also help. A teacher should include, as part of instruction, that details about this or that topic would be discussed at a later time, giving the time when it would happen, or a parent could set a future time for specific experiences. The inner aspect of looking forward to a specific experience is a valuable preparation for it. In this way wisdom becomes an active preparation for the future. The time horizon becomes expanded, which ultimately lead towards recognizing spiritual perspectives.

Justice, on the other hand, is something to be fought for throughout one's life, and if this sense of rightness, of the right orientation, is well developed in childhood, then that individual will no doubt do so. Eventually, in the course of human evolution, justice will become conscience. Examples of justice come in many forms, one being the form of stories.

Conclusion

Regarding courage and moderation, there is much more to explore beyond the brief perspectives presented in this essay. One fundamental aspect of the physical human body is the difference between our nervous system and our blood circulation.

This nerve substance is, so to speak, designed for life in the heavens, in the extraterrestrial realm, but because it is in our organism and has thus entered the earthly sphere, it dies. So we really have twelve senses. And from these twelve senses nerves extend into us like little trees. This is because the nervous system that belongs to our outer senses is the expression of the passage of the sun through the twelve constellations of the zodiac, which is symbolized in the relation of our entire nervous system to each of the twelve senses. Our nerve substance is entirely built up out of the heavens, out of the cosmos. It is alive in the heavens, in the cosmos, but it is dead in us because it has entered the earthly sphere.[24]

The nervous system, which in the prevailing scientific paradigm is responsible for our cognitive capacities, is, in reality an image of the cosmos, and its substance is dead, so that we may be able to think, that we may be able to have living thoughts in our souls—living thoughts leading towards wisdom.

Thus, because our nervous system lost its life in its descent into the earthly sphere, we carry an Ahrimanic element in us. And because our blood is alive—though by its very nature destined for death, that is, for mere chemical and physical processes—we have a Luciferic element in us. Ahriman can exist in us because our nervous system is dead, and because our blood is alive, Lucifer can live in us.[25]

Thus Ahriman works in us through all that is physical and prone to death forces: our pursuits of knowledge and wisdom and our sense of justice, all based on our physical body. Lucifer, on the other hand, works in us through our blood circulation, through exaggerating our heart forces, and also by intimidating the forces of moderation, so they cannot work as they should.

Therefore from the viewpoint of a teacher, whenever we encourage our students to practice the right timing of pursuits of knowledge, whenever we demonstrate through stories and examples that eventually justice will be done (if not in this life, then in the next, though this is not an appropriate theme for younger students), then we prepare them to stand strong against the influences of Ahriman, who would have us possess knowledge and justice immediately. Whenever we allow an element of consideration, of waiting for just the right moment to emerge, so that courage does not become foolhardiness and moderation does not give way to indulgence, then we prepare them to resist the influences of Lucifer.

When Steiner says that it is vital that in education the virtues of courage and moderation are promoted so that the students, children and adolescents do not bring sorrows on themselves, he means that whenever these virtues, as well as the other virtues, are reinforced through education and also in everyday life by parents or other adults in contact with children and adolescents, then in their preparation for the future they may take their own existence in hand consciously. He means for us to live in such a way today that one's future body is not compromised and thus becomes useless to one's spirit.

While at the present time it is not yet clear what the implications of morality are for the future of humanity, these will become evident eventually if we have confidence in spiritual guidance. Moral thinking, feeling and living mean to conceive of life, one's own and the ones of others, with the long view, with a spiritual perspective. Since the present-day Western worldview is mired in materialism, it will be necessary to expand this narrow viewpoint toward a real spiritual perspective for humanity. Steiner hints at that future:

> Our present cosmos is, regarding morality, neutral. The world of nature does not contain morality. However, a future world will come about that will express morality also in nature. Human beings carry their striving for morality into the future, to begin with towards their future incarnations, and so will become the agents for a future moral world in the course of time.[26]

ENDNOTES

1. Rudolf Steiner, paraphrased from *The Secret of Death in Relation to Middle Europe and Its Folk Spirits*, Lecture of January 31, 1915, Dornach: Rudolf Steiner Verlag, 2005.

2. About Plato's teachings on morality, see the *Politeia* and the *Nomoi* in works of Plato.

3. Steiner indicated in a number of his written works mental exercises towards the acquisition of impartiality, for instance the six exercises delineated in *Start Now! A Book of Soul and Spiritual Exercises*, edited by Christopher Bamford, Great Barrington, MA: SteinerBooks, 2004.

4. de Soto, Hernando. *The Mystery of Capital*, New York: Basic Books, 2000.

5. Steiner, Rudolf. *The Riddle of Humanity*, Lecture 5, London: Rudolf Steiner Press, 1990.

6. Op. cit., Steiner, *The Riddle of Humanity*, Lecture 6.

7. Steiner, Rudolf. *The Spiritual Foundation of Morality, Francis of Assisi and the Christ Impulse*, CW 155, Hudson, NY: Anthroposophic Press, 1995.

8. Op. cit., Steiner, *The Riddle of Humanity*.

9. For instance, a book discussing heart thinking is Florin Lowndes' book, *Enlivening the Chakra of the Heart*, New York: SteinerBooks, 2005.

10. *Report from Iron Mountain on the Possibility and Desirability of Peace*, New York: The Dial Press, Inc., 1967, p. 9.

11. Paraphrased from Rudolf Steiner, *The Secret of Death*, 12. Op. cit., Steiner, *The Riddle of Humanity*, Lecture 5.

13. Op. cit., Steiner, *The Spiritual Foundation of Morality*, Lecture 3.

14. Op. cit., Steiner, *The Riddle of Humanity*.

15. See also Rudolf Steiner, *The Spiritual Guidance of the Individual and Humanity*, CW 15, Hudson, NY: Anthroposophic Press, 1991.

16. Paraphrased from Rudolf Steiner, *The Secret of Death*, op. cit.

17. Ibid.

18. Ibid.

19. Op. cit., Steiner, *The Spiritual Foundation of Morality*.

20. Ibid.

21. Ibid.

22. Ibid.

23. Steiner discusses the sequence of cultural epochs in many works, for instance in *An Outline of Esoteric Science*, Great Barrington, MA: Anthroposophic Press, 1997.

24. Steiner, Rudolf. *Toward Imagination, Culture and the Individual*, Lecture 2, "Blood and Nerves," CW 169, Hudson, NY: Anthroposophic Press, 1990.

25. Ibid.

26. Paraphrased from Rudolf Steiner, *Philosophy, Cosmology and Religion in Anthroposophy*, Lecture 9, CW 215, Dornach: Rudolf Steiner Verlag, 1980.

The Third Challenge:
Answering Steiner's Call to Waldorf Teachers

Rather, the main difference in the effectiveness of teaching comes from the thoughts the teacher has had during the entire time of his or her existence and brings into the classroom....Above all, we must be conscious of the primary pedagogical task, namely that we must first make something of ourselves so that a living inner spiritual relationship exists between the teacher and the children.[1]

What does Steiner mean here? How do thoughts surround the individual, and how are they active? Earlier in this first lecture, after describing the human constituents and their relationship to the natural world as well as stages of future human evolution, Steiner charges teachers to ensure that children should breathe right, and then that they should sleep right, so that both their breathing rhythm and their day-night rhythm would support them well. Now, at the end of this lecture, Steiner points out that of primary significance is what the teacher is, not how many pedagogical tricks she or he knows. Among the many questions that arise from reading this first chapter, there are some about the nature of thought and its relationship with our personal development.

What Is a Thought?

A thought is quite unlike a physical entity. It is without physical dimensions, weight, quantity, or tangible measurements. If you compare a thought to a car, the car has weight, dimension, capacities, and a variety of devices that serve human beings well when driving this car. Of course, these devices were invented by human beings, who put their technical training to the task of making effective, efficient, and convenient vehicles.

A thought has, however, the possibility to permeate minds, and in so doing, inspire them. For instance, it has been proven many times historically that thinkers—scientists, philosophers—have had the same thought at the same time, although on different continents. Consequently, we cannot experience a thought the same way we experience a physical object, even if the physical object has been created by human thought.

How do we experience a thought? It lights up instantly in our soul configuration, our mind. Consider the process by which we access another person's thoughts. A thought can be expressed in words, on paper or spoken. We perceive the words, or read them. We then picture their meaning. We incorporate the thought into our own individual mind. Steiner points out that the capacity of thinking is inherited from our pre-birth existence in spiritual worlds, and that Descartes' famous words—*Cogito ergo sum*—are erroneous, because we experience thoughts as pictures, not as reality.[2] Thinking, as a purely non-physical, that is, spiritual, activity, enables us to move with our thoughts into this non-physical, that is, spiritual, realm.

It means that we both perceive and take into ourselves something that is distinctly non-physical. Thought, whether our own or somebody else's, is a clearly delineated entity of a non-physical essence, a clearly delineated body of meaning, despite its often material form, that is, its embodiment on paper, on a computer screen, or as speech sounds in the air. These are simply signs, symbols, and indicators of a thought. In our understanding we have to learn to decode written or spoken words in order to comprehend them.

We may also experience a thought even before it embodies itself in words. We probably have, as many others have too, experienced that a thought, an essence of meaning, an idea, has entered our awareness in a sudden and unexpected manner, like a lightning strike, or like a light bulb that suddenly comes on. In experience it is often exactly like a lightning strike—a sudden inspiration.

Human beings swim in the ocean of thought which exists all around us. We participate by forming our own thoughts, in separating our own thoughts from the ocean of thought around us, and also by taking in another individual's thoughts. Our souls, our minds, are permeable to this ocean of thought, whence ideas originate. It is sometimes even difficult to distinguish between our own and another person's thoughts. More on this further on.

Breathing Right

When we breathe in, we press in upon the brain fluid; when we exhale, it springs back into the body. In this way we transfer the breathing rhythm to the brain, and breathing is connected with nerve-sense life in the same way that it is connected with the metabolism. We can say that breathing is the most important human connection to the outer physical world.[3]

In this way Steiner describes that breathing links our metabolism with our sensory-nerve system, and thus truly unites us as human beings in an integrated entity. Steiner emphasizes that the first of the three essentials for Waldorf teachers is that their students must breathe right. Then this indicates that human beings in their souls and bodies, as well as their spirits, must be regarded as integrated individuals, instead of separating out each part of soul life.

If each part of soul life is separated, we come to phenomena common in today's world. I suggest here that in most of today's pedagogical systems the intellect is treated separately from the emotions, and both separately from an individual's will. A consequence of today's forms of education is that human beings find it very difficult to become integrated individuals, which also means that their soul forces—thinking, feeling and will—tend to act independently from each other. In today's society we meet the results of this separation often. When the soul forces act independently of each other, as separate entities, human beings have no moral stance. Therefore, we should not be surprised about the lack of morality evidenced in twentieth century civilization and its continuation into the twenty-first century.

There is another aspect which is related to the splitting of thinking from feeling, and both from the will nature of human beings.

You know that when we strive to enter the spiritual world, we must cross the threshold of this spiritual world. In the present epoch, the fifth post-Atlantean epoch, humanity has crossed this threshold, meaning that the three main activities of human soul life, that is thinking, feeling and will, have undergone a separation. As the whole of humanity has crossed this threshold, individuals may not be aware of this fact. It is simply an evolutionary necessity that this takes place.[4]

Steiner subsequently describes the necessity for today's humanity to order social structures according to the principles of the threefold social order, which we shall not discuss here. However, we begin to realize the consequences of this separation of thinking, feeling, and the independent will element of individuals, because through this separation the moral integrity of each person must become directed by the conscious spiritual entity that is the human "I," or eternal self.

Already in the 1890s Steiner foresaw this challenge to human beings, and so developed the means for individuals to learn the foresight necessary for what he called then moral imagination. We must learn consciously to foresee the consequences of our actions, and then deliberately act so as not to harm others.[5] In this way the human self participates actively in making choices.

Now, it appears that the work of the independent spiritual entity is made much more difficult in our age because of the above-mentioned facts. And so it becomes ever more vital that through education we help children who will have to work in this our world and will have to find their own moral compass as adults. Consequently, if education is permeated with right breathing, that is balance and harmony between the head and the limbs, and so engaging feeling in the right way, then we facilitate that students will become adults who will have found their moral direction, and thus will overcome as much as possible the split between thinking, feeling and will, which is the challenge of our age.

How can breathing be strengthened in a classroom situation? Most important of all is that teachers become aware of a breathing rhythm of classroom activities. Teachers should vary activities, for instance, not stick to intellectual bookwork for the whole length of a lesson, but call upon students to use artistic and movement activities to illustrate the intellectual content to be studied.[6] Steiner often stated that the classroom practice should become musical in essence, that one think of a lesson as variations on a theme, allowing students to experience the same content but in a variety of forms. In this way teaching supports right breathing.

Sleeping Right

Steiner regarded sleep as the uniting each night of the eternal self of each individual with her or his astral body—her or his consciousness/movement organization—in the spiritual world. Touching base with our spiritual essence might be a good description of sleep. Steiner even asserts that the spiritual beings who are most closely linked to human beings, the angels, archangels and archai, are in contact with us during sleep.[7] Upon waking we have no recollection of our spiritual meetings, but we do have impressions of either a restful and refreshing or a debilitating sleep experience.

For adults the questions are: What do we bring into sleep with us? Can we prepare our souls so that a rejuvenating sleep experience may follow? Can we rid our soul from the stresses and strains of daily life? Can we bring *presents* to these higher beings? Are these possibly positive thoughts and feelings? Are we burdened by negative thoughts and emotions? Steiner challenges all students of his worldview with the task to properly prepare for sleep, so that spiritual beings may indeed become a help to us. This, of course, is a matter for adults. Where children are concerned, we need to look for a different approach.

Right sleep preparation, in its simplest form, is a recollection of what we have experienced and done throughout the day, but bringing it to consciousness in reverse order. Steiner emphasizes the reverse order, because this reversal is inherent in what our life body, our ether body, does upon going to sleep. This review is often called the Review of the Day.[8] Steiner also points out that when executing a movement in the reverse order, or a line of reasoning, in actuality or thought such an exercise strengthens our ego, our independent spirit.

Obviously children and teenagers, who are not yet employing the full power of their essential self, their ego, cannot be expected to do the exercise of reviewing their day before going to sleep. What might be done by parents and teachers regarding children? One way is to do this for them. That means that when preparing for our own sleep, we actively present before our mind's eye what has happened this day with our charges. We then establish a spiritual relationship with them and take them into sleep with us.

What can teachers do in a classroom setting to help students experience a rejuvenating sleep experience? While as teachers there is very little that we can do directly, as we are not present when preparing children for sleep, we could describe a good preparation to parents. If we teach so that a spiritual view permeates all subjects, the children will already take the content of our teaching into sleep with them. As parents we can actually do quite a lot by preparing the going-to-bed occasion with a harmonious mood, reading to children at bed time, and, perhaps, speaking a prayer with them.

The most important issue required by Steiner of all Waldorf teachers nevertheless is that a real spiritual viewpoint permeate all that we do in the classroom. One aspect of preparing ourselves for sleep, that is meeting our own higher being while in spiritual realms, is to take our students with us. While we review our own day and our actions, we also picture our students. If we recognize the power of thought, if we recognize its cosmic existence and know of the ocean of thought within which all human beings live, then we know that by embracing students in picture, by including them in our sleep preparation, we are united with them in the great ocean of cosmic being, whence all life-giving thoughts arise. The reality of this sleep connection may be proven to us when preparing a difficult exercise with our classes. For instance, when planning to introduce a difficult movement exercise to the class, I have often found it very useful to imagine, in as much detail as possible, that same exercise the day before. I would run through my explanation, through my actions, through the precise actions of the students. The next day, when actually working on this exercise in physical reality, I would notice that the thought preparation of the previous night had helped a great deal.

In its simplest form, while we review the day, actually run from end to beginning, we may picture the class of students we teach, and then— briefly—picture every student in turn, possibly in their seats. What they wore this day, how they behaved this day, any special comments they made, or we made to them. In other words, to put before us a brief picture of their physical appearance and behavior. It is this image that we take with us into sleep. For the sake of our own sanity and well-being, and with a little practice, we learn to picture the students in seconds and avoid long drawn out memories.

This practice also builds up our own spiritual relationship with our students. However, are there ways in which we may help them towards their own refreshing sleep experiences?

In our teaching it is also essential that we also describe a variety of historical or even imagined persons who are able to accomplish important feats of courage or righteousness. It is vital that models of human beings who follow an upright path are portrayed as vividly as possible. In many Waldorf schools teachers of the upper grades, not necessarily in high school, whenever the subject matter is not history or literature (which contain many a worthy example), may take a few minutes at the end of main lesson to tell a story, to use this time to describe dramatically, pictorially and colorfully such role models, whether they are historical individualities or imagined persons, for the sake of telling a tale for its therapeutic effect. Teachers hope that such tales will so stir the imagination of their students that the stories told will accompany the students into sleep. It means also that it is important for teachers to develop their storytelling skills. If the human beings portrayed for students are strong, forceful and upright individuals, then from the teacher's viewpoint much has been done to enhance a student's harmonious entry into sleep. If a student is truly moved by hearing about individuals of spiritual, historical or emotional significance, then her or his astral body will carry intense pictures into sleep, and her or his ego will expand them. In such a way role models may come to play an important part in the impending shape of morality as the student becomes an adult.

> What human beings receive from the higher worlds comes to them during sleep.[9]

A Living Inner Spiritual Relationship

The comments on the importance of breathing and sleeping already describe a spiritual relationship between a teacher and her or his students. One might even say that the intentions of teachers to help their students to breathe right helps them to find a relationship to the ether world of living entities, for, after all, breath unites us with all other living beings. Moreover, we might realize that when we help students to sleep healthfully by finding a relationship to higher beings, their astral bodies, their consciousness-movement organizations are helped. Now, when we attempt to find a truly spiritual relationship to our students, then our own self must find a way to consciously relate to each student's self. An ego-to-ego relationship exists when we forego the usual relationship of adult to child, when we forego the feeling that we know more, are more capable, and have progressed further in knowledge of the world than the students we teach. A certain amount of humility, which recognizes that in each student lie hidden gifts of past and future karma that we, as their teachers, are privileged to help manifest, will promote the right spiritual relationship with our students.

Above all we need to develop the awareness that it is an illusion to think that we are separated from others through the confines of our physical body, through our skin. On the contrary, we are in continuous relationship with other human beings, with spiritual beings, with some elements of the natural world that are alive via all portions of our human organization that are not physical and material. The human ether body (our life organism), the human astral body (our consciousness/movement organization, what might be called our soul configuration), and our eternal self (our ego) are spread out in the ocean of thought and spirit that surrounds the earth and all of humanity. While our consciousness is confined to the experiences of our physical body, the sense impressions, and our memories, the depths of our own being are far wider, deeper and considerably more spiritual than our physical existence can indicate. Consequently, when I said above that we swim in an ocean of thought, a cosmic ocean of creative thought, we should acknowledge this reality and thus guide our own thinking in such a way that we deliberately avoid negative thoughts, so we do not project a maelstrom of destructive energies into the cosmic surrounding. It is quite a task in today's world to transform thoughts to become constructive positions, as there exists much that invites negative and destructive positions. Much inner effort is required to achieve this.

To give a personal example: Quite a while ago I had the experience of being particularly annoyed by the attitudes and behavior of one of my colleagues in the Waldorf school where I was teaching. At a certain point I realized that this negative attitude was not helpful, and so over several nights, I attempted to change my attitude by recognizing that person's positive characteristics. A verse of Steiner's helped me to do so. I did this work at night in preparation for going to sleep. After several days I experienced that this person's attitude toward me also seemed to have changed, which was confirmed by his responses to me. In short, the work I was doing in my own soul had twofold positive results.

It is a hard exercise of self-knowledge to rid our souls of negativity, of disgust, of doubt, and perhaps hatred for others, and convert these soul energies into a positive direction. When we accept the fact that the whole of humanity is in fact a brotherhood, and that at times events occur that might be unpleasant for the moment but in the end prove to move us forward in our attempts at self development, we may be moved to give thanks to those who have appeared to oppose us but have indirectly helped us.

In actuality, there are fundamental changes beginning to happen in the present stage of humanity's evolution regarding our experience of our own self. They begin today in preparation for the next stage of evolution and can be somewhat disturbing for our present-day experience.

Does the man of today not find his ego, then? No, he does not find it...for the true ego comes to a stop when we are born. What we experience of our ego is only a reflection of it...But this real ego, which could be found during the time of atavistic clairvoyance and into the early Christian era, will not be found today by looking into man's own being—in as far as this being is united with the body. Only indirectly does he experience something of his ego, when he comes into relation with other people, and his karma comes into play.

If we meet another person, and something takes place between us connected with our karma, then something of the impulse of our true ego enters into us...It is characteristic of the age of the consciousness soul that the human being has his ego only as a reflection, so that he may enter into the age of the spirit self and be able to experience the ego again in a new form—a different form... They [human beings] will have to accustom themselves, however, to seeing this ego only in the outer world.[10]

It is indeed through the actions and attitudes of others that we may sense our own essence—not an easy task in the present conditions which tend to obfuscate the essence of humanity.

I once said recently that anyone can discover the truth by calling to mind his biography, factually, and asking himself what he owes since birth to this person or that. In this way he will slowly and gradually resolve himself into influences coming from others; and he will find extraordinarily little in what he usually considers his real ego, which is really only its reflection, as has been said.[11]

Following these recommendations by Steiner will allow us to place ourselves rightly into the community of fellow workers and elucidate our responsibilities towards ourselves and others, and particularly towards our charges. It is essential to include the students we teach in this community of individuals around us, for in them is active already what they, before birth, have taken on as their specific tasks in this very life. While it may be difficult to accept, it is a reality that children in general, and our students in particular, may teach us a great deal. Actually it is a very valid and significant experience whenever we know that we have learned from children. They, after all, have left the spiritual world more recently than we have.

Conclusion

One of the questions raised by Steiner's imperative direction for teachers in the beginning of his lectures to prospective Waldorf teachers has to do with morality. What is it that constitutes a moral stance in all human beings?

The first capacity we must learn is to orient our body in space.[12]

Steiner goes on to describe what happens during the first three years. He relates the capacity of uprightness (and indirectly the capacities of speaking and thinking) to the concept of Justice—one of four virtues described by Plato.

Finally, the virtue which is the most spiritual, and has connection with the whole human being, is the virtue of uprightness, of justice. We possess this virtue in the first years of childhood only. We then develop the capacity to lift up our head, and the forces of uprightness also enable us to speak. Finally, when we think we are in touch with the forces of wisdom pervading the whole cosmos. This force of uprightness, of righteousness, is a gift of the cosmos, pointing us to past incarnations.[13]

He describes justice—uprightness—as having begun as a gift of the cosmos on Ancient Saturn (Steiner describes previous formations of the body of the earth, among others what he calls Ancient Saturn, Ancient Sun, and Ancient Moon[14]), but undergoing a transformation in our Earth Evolution, and finally coming to fulfillment in the far distant future of what he calls the Vulcan Evolution.[15]

This capacity of uprightness, of justice, as it penetrates the beginning of human life, not only indicates spiritual forces active in all human beings, but also indicates their spiritual nature. In order to help human beings develop to the best of their abilities, to the best to which they aspire, it is imperative that the adults around growing children and the teachers who teach growing children have not only an appreciation of the spiritual nature of all individuals, but actively pursue all avenues of bettering themselves. I am reminded that in a far distant age, at the time of Zoroaster, the teaching of

> The Good Word,
> The Good Thought and
> The Good Deed

was promulgated. In these three moral aspirations the element of justice is present. It throws a vital light on the ancient civilization of Iran, of Persia, which saw the origin of Zoroastrianism. In this civilization, of which only much later and often incomplete writings exist, there was much evidence of an understanding of humanity's relationship to spiritual worlds, to spiritual beings and of humanity's task on the earth. For instance, by exercising the good word, thought and deed, human beings would drive away the demons that would prey on them, lie to them and lead them astray. The tenets of this Zoroastrian religion, while not appropriate for our time, were fundamental towards the development of humanity. When speaking about the evolution of mankind, Steiner states that a repetition of human attitudes towards spiritual worlds will again occur in the epoch of human development following our own.

While I do not wish to infer that in our age we should practice Zoroastrianism, it might be good to remember that the potential for a moral compass, the stance of uprightness in word, deed and thought, has been given to all human beings, and that it is the responsibility of all adults surrounding children, parents and teachers alike, to help develop this potential further than the gift of the first years of life.

I hope that I have demonstrated why Steiner places such emphasis on developing our own self as far as is given to us in our particular life situation if we wish to work with children and adolescents.

> We need to make our thoughts very concrete; we need to form our thoughts so that we can be conscious that this school fulfills something special. We can do this only when we do not view the founding of this school as an everyday occurrence, but instead regard it as a ceremony held within Cosmic Order.[16]

ENDNOTES

1. Steiner, Rudolf, *Foundations of Human Experience*, Lecture 1, CW 293, Hudson, NY: Anthroposophic Press, 1996.

2. Op. cit., Steiner, Lecture 2.

3. Op. cit., Steiner, Lecture 1.

4. Paraphrased from Rudolf Steiner, *Past and Future Impulses for Social Development*, CW 190, Lecture of April 11, 1919.

5. Steiner, Rudolf. *Intuitive Thinking as a Spiritual Path*, CW 4, New York: Anthroposophic Press, 1995.

6. Of course there are numerous books by experienced Waldorf teachers describing many of their methods. I have described many examples of this in my previous books *The Temperaments and the Arts* and *Awakening Intelligence*, Fair Oaks, CA: AWSNA Publications, 2003.

7. Steiner describes these contacts in many of his works.

8. Reference to this and other spiritual exercises may be found in *Start Now! A Book of Soul and Spiritual Exercises* by Rudolf Steiner, edited by Christopher Bamford, SteinerBooks, 2004.

9. Op. cit., Steiner, *Foundations of Human Experience*.

10. Steiner, Rudolf. *How Can Mankind Find the Christ Again?* Lecture of December 27, 1918, CW 187, Hudson, NY: Anthroposophic Press, 1947.

11. Ibid.

12. Steiner, Rudolf. *The Spiritual Guidance of the Individual and Humanity*, Chapter 1, CW 15, New York: Anthroposophic Press, 1991.

13. Paraphrased from Rudolf Steiner, *The Secret of Death*, CW 159, Lecture of January 31, 1915.

14. Steiner, Rudolf. *An Outline of Esoteric Science*, CW 13, New York: SteinerBooks, 1997.

15. Steiner, Rudolf. *The Riddle of Humanity*, Lecture of August 6, 1916, London: Rudolf Steiner Press, 1990.

16. Op. cit., Steiner, *Foundations of Human Experience*, Opening Address.

Organizations as Living Organisms

Introduction: Developing a Seven-Fold View

In this essay I would like to develop a view of Waldorf schools and other organizations that honor the reality of human individuals as beings of body, soul, and spirit. I must make it clear that I am not a management or organizational expert. Rather, I have life-long experience working in the Camphill movement and in a number of Waldorf schools throughout the world. So my viewpoint is that of a person dealing with developing and adult human beings.

I am hoping that the picture I develop in this paper will, ideally, be taken up and worked with by all persons intimately involved in a school or other organization—the people in managerial and administrative positions, faculty, and recipients of services, such as parents in a school and clients or customers in a business organization. The picture of a healthy, and therefore living, organism needs to be seen in the context of a specific place, time, and structure. Several rounds of conversations may be needed before a specific picture emerges with respect to the matrix of the ideal I will describe. Consequently, it may take further rounds of conversation to outline an appropriate approach to reshape the organization so that it becomes healthy or can maintain its present good health.

It is habit among those involved with anthroposophical institutions to speak in human terms about organizations such as Waldorf schools and other institutions inspired by Rudolf Steiner's philosophy. Comparisons are often made between human and organizational phases of growth and development. These are all well and good comparisons, but communities of men and women working together may develop over much longer periods of time than a human life span. Moreover, the interaction matrix of an organization is much more complex than a single human life. Think of a city, a nation!

Therefore, I would like to propose a different model for looking at the living time profile of an organism or organization. I do so not because I believe previous models are wrong or because I think that applying human phases of development to organizations is erroneous, but because I believe that an organization that is meant to be living must be measured against and spoken about in terms of the forces of life.

The forces of life are manifest in greatest purity in the world of plants. Each plant manifests in some form or other the following aspects: its rootedness in the ground; the intake and flow of liquid and subsequent transformation; an air exchange with its surroundings; a reaction to warmth; a reaction to light; a manifestation of geometrical, mathematical principles (also inherent in sound and music); and finally, the crowning profile of a living organism, life itself. Air, Water, Fire, and Earth are the traditionally acknowledged life-sustaining elements. Three others need to be added: Light, Form, and Life. These are the seven principles which I suggest may lead one to a clearer understanding of the health and well-being of a human organization. I shall describe these elements from the viewpoint of a tree and also from the viewpoint of a group of individuals working together. I shall conclude with some comments on gatherings, meetings, and organs of a living organism.

The Seven-Fold Picture in Its Living Manifestation

When looking at a tree, one can divide its form into roots, trunk, and crown and assign to each its function; that is one way of understanding. If, however, we follow the seven life principles in their activity in sustaining the tree in its totality, then we arrive at a different picture. If we track the activity of individuals in different areas of an organization by using the first picture and determine that one person works at the root of the organizational tree, another at the level of the trunk, and a third at the crown, then we fix each person's level of involvement. This is done routinely in various organizational charts that separate out, prioritize and describe the functions of different people or groups involved in an enterprise. Organizational charts include various interconnections and overlaps of positions and departments. Applied to a Waldorf school these might include the faculty, administration, board, parents, committees, and so forth.

Problems in a school often arise, however, because people feel themselves chained to or restricted by others to a particular area by their job description. In reality human beings participate—consciously and unconsciously—in all areas of an enterprise and are likewise affected by all areas. The opportunity of freeing individuals from their narrow functional confines so that they may become more active participants in the growth and nurture of their organizational "tree" is my goal in presenting the following picture of sevenfold life activity.

The Solid, Earth Element

The earth provides a firm basis for a tree's roots, enabling the tree to grow at a particular place at a particular time. A tree's roots, together with the firm ground, represent the physical plant or the buildings and grounds of a school or other institution. An organization should have a deep taproot—a main building—and smaller service roots and rootlets, which help it to penetrate deeply into the community. In a school, an off-site kindergarten or a performing arts venue, for instance, can serve as such additional roots.

The earth element in an organization is the extent to which a school is literally grounded and has its own place in the physical world, a permanent location, in other words, whether an organization has really sunk its roots into the physical world. It also shows whether the tree—the mission or impulse of the organization—has rooted itself in suitable soil. The specific qualities of the ground may also significantly influence the way an "organizational tree" is able to connect with the physical world and itself in a particular location. Sand, clay, granite, limestone—all influence the roots of a tree quite differently.

The characteristic signature of the earth element is a square or crystalline form; its spatial dimensions tend to be compressed and concentrated, and its time signature is a slow and carefully stepped growth pattern. It is hardy, however, and once established, will likely last for years.

The Liquid, Water Element

The liquid element enables the life giving forces and substances to permeate a tree in order to sustain and foster growth. As it courses through all parts of a tree, the liquid element itself is changed, eventually transformed into vapor and released into the atmosphere. As it rises and falls in the sap and evaporates through the leaves to join the atmosphere, the water element is a symbol and picture of the flow of money and its transformation through the organization. The money stream that surges or trickles through the  organizational tree provides a picture of money circulation, its availability, its procurement and source, and finally, the areas it stimulates when rejoining the general atmosphere.

The different sources of water, such as groundwater or an aquifer, or its absence can be seen as a variety of money sources, as the general monetary constitution of the community at large. A water-rich, year-round river close to the school may be a reliable and continuous cash supply, while a seasonal stream may create a great struggle for survival.

The characteristic water signature is a half-moon shape, which indicates both a tendency to spread out and fill all available space and a strong cyclical quality in its time dimension of growth and development, thus uniting regular and seasonal activity. A school or other organization may be, for instance, like a tree that needs water but lives in a desert, or a tree that is established in a region with an ample aquifer but is prevented from reaching it by deep layers of rock. These are but two possibilities that need close scrutiny by those who are part of the organization. In the first instance there may be ample money in the community, but the mode of access has yet to be found.

The Gaseous, Airy Element

The air surrounding a tree is altered by the tree's metabolism in hourly, daily, monthly, and yearly cycles. The air element represents the atmosphere of the community surrounding the school tree. Both water and air elements are connected to the leaves of the tree. The quality of the air and subsequently

the condition of the leaves show how positively or negatively the larger community acts towards the school. The airy element is intimately connected to the light. With the help of light, trees take in carbon dioxide during the day, and they give off oxygen at night. This life-giving element of oxygen enlivens the whole community.

The quality of air affects the growth of a tree. Smog-filled air, for example, may be poisonous to trees, while clean air fosters healthy growth and development. Ocean air is different from mountain air, desert air, or air rich with tropical forest humidity. Moreover, there are innumerable types of air currents, depending on the typical weather patterns of a region: regular refreshing breezes, tropical storms, polar winds, hurricanes or monsoons, and localized wind patterns in great variety. The characteristic signature of the air element is its tendency to form triangular, arrowhead shapes. In its great expansiveness, it fills all available space. It is also fickle and capriciously changeable, volatile and irregular in its tempo of development. One of the vital points for the health of the school tree is whether the surrounding atmosphere is filled with light and clean air or is continually murky and polluted.

The Warmth Element

Warmth works in diverse ways on different levels of life and organization. It fills the atmosphere with its expanding quality to bring flowers and seeds into existence so that the future of a tree may be ensured. A school tree needs the warmth of the good will of  the whole school community as well as that of the greater community in which it exists. Likewise, it needs the internally active warmth element within so that children, teachers, and parents may bring their good will to bear to create seeds for the future. The warmth element is pervasive and needs to permeate all areas of the organism, for it carries the human element of will into all the other functions.

Questions regarding the working of the warmth element are crucial to the well-being of the organism: when and how it is created; who is able to create it; who benefits from it; and, most importantly, if it is possible to have too much warmth. The focus and direction of the warmth of the will is a vital consideration for the healthy functioning of an organism such as a Waldorf school. Are there frequent periods of intense warmth, when a great deal is accomplished, interspersed with benign rest periods? Or is there a continuous blast of a furnace, stoked by certain individuals, which threatens to burn up and destroy most individuals' impulses and never allows for rest and recuperation? Is there perennial cold, which makes every smallest initiative a painful process of exertion?

The essential signature of the warmth element is its capacity to permeate everything and unite all objects formed by the other elements—even all humanity—in a great sphere of warmth. The form and spatial dimension of warmth is spherical. As regards temporal development patterns, warmth always thrusts forward in expansion unless stopped by cooler elements.

The capacity to lay the foundation for the future is bound up with the specific working of the warmth element around and within the organizational tree. Warmth works to manifest the fruits of the past and the seeds for the future. It is probably the most difficult element to control, focus, and harness, since it springs spontaneously from the hearts of human beings inspired by their mission and work, and thus has a far wider range into the surrounding community than the other elements.

The Element of Light

The light element permeates atmospheric warmth and air insofar as they are not suffused by water in the form of clouds, mist, or fog. The light element penetrates liquids depending on their nature; clear water allows light to permeate completely, although it bends the beams of light. Light bounces off the surfaces of opaque, solid matter. But if the material is transparent or translucent, it allows light to pass through, though usually with some refraction.

What does the light element of an organization represent, and what is the source of this light? Since ancient times light has been equated with wisdom and knowledge. The light element in an organization such as a Waldorf school has its source in the pedagogical knowledge and insights of the faculty. The pedagogical research of individual faculty members, over and above the work of the whole faculty, contributes to this source. The receptivity of the "solid substances" and "denser elements" in a community determines whether the light of wisdom and knowledge is able to shine out and become a beacon to its community or whether the light is kept under a bushel basket and hidden from public view.

Let us clarify the relationship of light to the physical elements. A source of light needs continuous renewal and regeneration. The striving for knowledge and insight, the search for deepening and ever-honing one's thinking capacities—whether one's immediate task is as an individual or as part of a group, as a parent, teacher, or board member—feeds the light. To keep the source pure and shining is no easy task, for light may be perverted to become splintered or dehumanized. If this happens, and insights are applied egotistically for personal advantage, then beams of light become thorns to pierce the hearts and souls of others. Intellectual arrogance has a most detrimental effect on one's colleagues or coworkers. Then light may harden into wounding intellectualism, which is a consequence of the selfish use of wisdom and knowledge.

Communication is necessary so that light can literally enlighten interactions with others and not impose barriers. When light becomes too physical—too strong or too great a sensitivity—a plant will actually produce thorns. Those individuals in an organization who are quite sensitive to the quality of the light that streams out will know if management is impervious and closes itself off or if a school's faculty insist that they "know better."

Light should permeate the warmth of good will and direct its actions meaningfully. Light should also be able to shine out into the airy atmosphere of the greater community. There it may meet many obstacles and obstructions in the form of murky or polluted atmosphere. Water and liquid—representing the money stream of an organization—may be transparent and permeable by the light of insight and wisdom, but if it carries too much silt and other impurities, they may block out the light. Even in clear water the direction of light gets refracted.

Solid matter—unless translucent or transparent—does not allow light to enter, but reflects it on its surface. Human beings need to transform matter through the arts to make it light-permeable. One example is lazured wall surfaces, which allow the inhabitants of a room to feel able to penetrate the solidity of the walls. Likewise, architectural forms determine how the light of insight and wisdom may shine within a building and likewise ray out of the building into the community.

A non-material element such as light considerably modifies the effects of the denser elements. Through the element of light, the wisdom of Waldorf pedagogy is made visible. This source of wisdom is nurtured and strengthened by the working of the faculty to deepen their knowledge and continue their research into the essence of what is human.

The Element of Sound and Number Relationships

This element is even more elusive than light. It stands in polarity to the watery/fluid element, and some of its effects are quite mysterious. The inner music of an organization or school demonstrates the working together of colleagues, coworkers, and administration. The pattern of communal working for the greater good and the shared vision literally resound in the symphony of an organism's inner music. Its harmony, or disharmony, is heard and perceived by the greater community and provides a potent tool for judging the organization's health and well-being.

Sound reverberates and echoes in the physical elements and sets them in motion. The internal working of the faculty of a school or of the management of a company is heard by all who are connected to the institution, not with physical ears, but with the ears of the soul and mind. Is there a rousing song or a repetitious, boring, tune? Is there a tune at all or only confusing noise? Is there complete silence or an enthralling harmony, an orchestra or a chorus? It is Elvis Presley or the Rolling Stones, reggae or rap, Bach or Mozart?

The signature tune of a school or organization is one of its vital components, but one most often ignored. It can be transformed. An instrument may be tuned, an orchestra may learn to play together in the same key and measure, and individualistic loners or prima donnas may in time learn to make music in harmony with others.

The character of a school's music will greatly determine its ability to attract money. A great and rousing symphony will be heard far and wide in the greater community and attract attention and approval. A pure but harmonious tune will be heard, like a songbird's mellifluous tune transcending the roar of traffic, but it may only reach the immediate neighborhood. Disharmony will annoy those who hear it and will cause the flow of money to diminish to a trickle.

Just as the water element has a strongly periodic and seasonal flow and ebb, so does the inner music. Sound and liquids are inherently related. Different tunes are appropriate for different seasons. Different forms of income are also appropriate for different seasons, for different objectives.

Just as it is important to determine the character of an organization's music, so it is also essential to determine the character of its audience. Playing Mozart at a rock concert may not bring about much listening or enthusiasm. The music of the environment, of the audience, is as important as that of the internal social relationship.

Who creates this internal music? Primarily the individuals involved and responsible for the organization's mission, management, and operation. If these individuals recognize each other's humanity, especially acknowledging each other as spiritual beings striving to manifest their best and most honest work and to overcome personal prejudices and difficulties for the benefit of the whole, then harmony and music will arise. Steiner has given many indications about how to develop one's inner, spiritual capacities, not only for oneself, but also for the benefit of the social organism. If these indications are truly worked with on a regular basis, and—in the case of a school—if they live in the souls of the faculty, board, and parents, then a school's inner music is enhanced, and members of the community will begin to be in tune with each other.

The Element of Life

A living organism is viable when all the essential elements of life are ordered and integrated to form a self-sustaining, healthy organism. The life of an organization such as a school depends on the spiritual striving of its members. If teachers take their commitment to anthroposophy and Waldorf education seriously enough and work on their inner development, or if they are members of a college of teachers, or of the School of Spiritual Science and its Pedagogical Section, then they infuse life and the potential of organic order into their respective schools. Correspondingly, the spiritual striving of the directors and managers of a company whose goals extend beyond economic success to serve social ideals will also act as a spiritual core of their organization.

In the larger community there are also those individuals who are striving spiritually, who support the impulse and initiative of an organization with spiritual goals much like a Waldorf school's by recognizing that their service is to the true image of the human being. Then their contributions will strengthen the existence of their school, organization or business and help its impulse to be rooted in fertile ground.

We have come full circle. It is apparent that there is a reciprocal relationship between the ideal and spiritual initiatives and the practical rootedness in physical manifestation—namely in the physical plant, housing, building, or property which the organization owns or hopes to own. The stronger the spiritual impulse and commitment, the better the opportunities for physical expression.

Concluding Remarks: the Element of Time

When dealing with a living organism such as a plant, we should also consider its life and organs in the context of its time signature. Growth occurs in spurts, not in constant graduated increases, and is characterized by expansive as well as contractive processes. Just as one may see in a plant nodes of contraction at crucial points, such as the location from which expansion into leaves and blossoms begins, one may also recognize such nodes in an organization. These organizational nodes represent a concentration of energies created through the work of individuals to serve the organism as a whole and to help it develop harmoniously and productively.

Before expansion is possible, a phase of contractive, concentrated, and focused deliberate planning and imagining activity has to occur. A seed is the ultimate contractive form: it contains the potential for the entire future plant or organism. As the proverb says, "Out of small acorns mighty oaks do grow." It is important to be clear about what is needed for a precious seed of intention to grow into reality and what physical, soul, and spiritual conditions are fostered by the attention of the individuals involved in the process.

The organs in an organization such as a school are the groups that meet regularly, occasionally, sporadically, or just once for a specific purpose. If we honor the time signature of a living organism, we shall be careful not to endow groups with perpetuity, for then no development can take place. We shall also not fix individuals even semi-permanently as carriers of such group activity, for this would counteract development, which needs to be open-ended, and also deprive individuals of their own freedom to develop themselves.

Moreover, we should be wary of viewing the time signature of organizations in terms of human life phases because we could create a pattern that does not correspond to the life principle of organizations. For example, while Steiner pointed repeatedly to the law of seven-year cycles in human lives, he also pointed to a thirty-three-year cycle of social and historical life, and to a much larger three-hundred-fifty-year cycle of paradigm shifts in historical development. The thirty-three-year cycle, for instance, is repeated three times in a century, with a phase of impulse and intention which then becomes manifest in society if the impulse was forceful enough. I am inclined to regard the life cycles of organizations as much longer than those of individual men and women.

Let us consider an organization that wants to be alive by manifesting the seven elements described above and that has a healthy succession of expansion and contraction in the formation of its organs. Such an organization would not fix individuals into any set positions because individuals need to be free to be active in one of the organs of the organization for a time but not forever.

It is important for each organ of the organization to have a clear purpose and mandate. Further, the smallest possible number of persons is usually the most efficient group or committee. Rotation of duties, too, is a good idea, so that everyone is actively engaged and the load is evenly distributed. Time limits for meetings need to be kept. If the group is a special-purpose group, it should be dissolved after its purpose is achieved. If it is a permanent group with a clear purpose, the application of Waldorf classroom dynamics—such as changes of tempo and activity within the meeting time—will help ensure that members remain fresh and focused on the tasks.

Above all, it is important to consider the reciprocity of the seven life elements and how they can enhance each other. They can also interfere and hinder healthy development of an organization if no attention is paid to their inherent character and their relationship to time. In this essay I have attempted to describe a process involving the seven life-sustaining forces and how they pertain to the health of a school or other organization. Holding this living picture in mind can help us to visualize an organization's particular challenges and strengths allowing it to become a more healthy organism.

"Organizations as Living Organisms: Developing a Seven-fold View" first appeared in the *Research Bulletin*, Vol. VII, No. 2, Spring, 2002.

The Seven Cosmic Artists:
An Artistic View of Child Development

But what power expresses itself through imagination? To understand this, let us look at childhood. Free, creative imagination does not yet live and manifest in the child…. [I]magination lies hidden in the child; he is actually full of it. In the shaping of his own organism the child is inwardly the most significant sculptor. The child is also a musical artist, for he tunes his nerve strands in a distinctly musical fashion. To repeat: Power of imagination is power to grow and harmonize the organism.[1]

Waldorf education, education that follows the understanding of Rudolf Steiner, has as its basis a particular view of the human being as a being of body, soul, and spirit. In many of his lectures to teachers and prospective teachers in Waldorf schools, Steiner emphasized that we cannot understand Waldorf education unless we look at the human being from the viewpoint of spiritual science. We need to look at human beings as living before birth in spiritual worlds and as having lived a previous life on earth incarnated in a human body of flesh and blood. Moreover, after death human beings will again sojourn in realms of spirit and work on their future lives and future tasks. They will do this both with the human souls with whom they share a destiny and with angelic beings, beings who are more highly developed than are human beings at this particular stage of earth evolution.

This view leads to a view of child development that is different from a traditional one. Processes that we may observe in early childhood, the elementary school years, adolescence, and early adulthood gain a different emphasis. Encouraged by several of Steiner's remarks, I would like to propose in this paper one particular way of considering this process of development.

In a lecture of December 29, 1914, Steiner brought the arts into relationship with the essential human being, including those parts or bodies that are already developed at this time and those that are in preparation for future development, as follows:

Art	Respective Human Body
Architecture	Physical Body
Sculpture	Life Body (Ether Body)
Painting	Consciousness or Movement Body (Astral Body)
Music	Ego (Eternal Self)
Poetry	Spirit Self (not yet fully developed)
Eurythmy	Life Spirit (not yet developed)
The Seventh Art	Spirit Human (not yet developed) [2]

Steiner discussed how one part of the human essence, for instance the ether body or life body, works down into the more perfected part, in this case the physical body, and that a mode of the respective art is used in that interaction. For example, the life body works into the physical body using sculptural principles. Life principles of the ether body transform the art of sculpture into the physical body of a living entity. The physical body itself, through architecture, uses the materials and structural laws—such as gravity—of the external, physical, natural world. When we look at the higher constituent parts of the human being, however, much development lies far in the future. Steiner declared at the end of this lecture that, in the future, yet other arts, at present not yet imaginable, will come into being.

The above schema provides the signposts for understanding child development. I will elaborate on how this is so in the following pages.[3]

Developmental Periods

Steiner frequently mentions developmental periods of about seven years in length, but he also mentions divisions of each of these seven-year periods into thirds of roughly two-and-a-third years each.[4] I propose that in the middle of each of these seven-year cycles an event of great significance occurs, one that manifests in the acquisition of new faculties.[5] The middle period of each seven-year cycle invites a Cosmic Artist to begin working on the incarnation of the child into her or his body. Each such event marks the gentle beginning of an essential aspect of human development. These new faculties in human life inspire artists and, when seen in the light of child development, they hint also at the broadening and deepening of human capacities and perception in general. During these middle periods, as well as at the beginning of each seven-year cycle, a new feeling quality, a balancing quality—essentially an artistic quality—arises.

Cosmic artistic forces that accord with the art and artistic quality at work become effective every three-and-one-half years and last in initial impact for seven years. These cosmic artistic impulses continue on in life and, in some cases, manifest in a simple form earlier than we might predict. They set faculties in motion, initiated at certain points of a child's or adolescent's life and impart specific capacities. Once these capacities are born, it is up to the individual to foster and develop them.

1. The Cosmic Being of Architecture: Cosmic Morphology

From whence does the newborn child receive its human form? From whence come imperfections and gifts?[6] From whence comes the matter that builds up a human body? An individual prepares his or her particular form—with help from the spiritual world—before birth. As Steiner indicated:

> Here on earth we carry a body made of bones, muscles, arteries and so forth. Then, after death, we acquire a spiritual body, formed

out of our moral qualities. For what lies inside of man is the whole spiritual cosmos in condensed form. In man's inner organism we have an image of the entire cosmos...The human being, who has undergone after death all the states described by me previously, now becomes manifest to the vision of Man himself. The human being is a spirit among spirits. Yet, what he sees now as his world is the marvel of the human organism itself in the form of the universe, the whole cosmos. Just as on earth we build machines, keep accounts, sew clothes, make shoes or write books, thus weaving together what is called the content of civilization, of culture, so above, together with the spirits of the higher Hierarchies and incorporeal human beings, we weave the woof and weft of mankind. We weave mankind out of the cosmos. Here on earth we appear as finished products. There we lay down the spiritual germ of earthly man.[7]

Steiner's views, considered objectively, can help our understanding of what is happening during a child's first moments, weeks, and months after birth. From the moment of birth, many influences bear on us, including influences from our physical and psychological environments. A child's own forces, however, hidden deeply within her or his being, take hold of the body and form it to its purpose.

Spiritual forces shape our physical being. The Cosmic Being of Architecture helps human beings to shape the "houses" within which they will lead their lives. Just as a house or a place of business or worship has particular structures—such as windows, doors, plumbing—our body, as the temple of our soul, also has particular features.[8] For this reason I consider the cosmic forces that underlie architecture as the first formative forces for human beings. I deliberately use the word *cosmic* because these forces are active prior to birth. Architecture makes use of physical building materials, but architecture also requires detailed plans in order for builders to construct a building. The work that human souls undergo and in which they participate in spiritual worlds between earth lives may be seen as the making of architectural plans. We find elements of the physical world in the human body, but they are placed organically, marvelously, according to a plan.

Hence the body, the envelope of the soul, which clothes the ego, which is inhabited by the ego, is described as the temple of the ego within, the temple of the divinity dwelling in man, the temple of God. When, therefore, you form this body, you are building a future temple, that is to say, the new incarnation of the Earth.[9]

2. Perfecting the Human Body: The Cosmic Sculptor

Children do not merely grow, they also perfect the forms of their bodies. These forms become ever more capable of fulfilling human capacities, such as upright, balanced posture, speech, and personal memory and thinking.

[A] supersensible contemplation of man will reveal to us, apart from his physical body, another finer body which we have called the ether body or the body of formative forces. From this ether body spring not only all the forces sustaining nourishment and growth, but it is also the source of the faculties of remembering and of making mental images, of ideation. It becomes an independent entity only during the change of teeth, at which time it is born in a way similar to the physical birth of its body from its mother. This means that up to the change of teeth the forces of the ether body are working entirely in the processes of the child's organic growth, and after that time—though still remaining active in this realm to a great extent—they partly withdraw from these activities. If we observe the gradual withdrawal of some of these ether forces until approximately the seventh year, we can see how in the first two-and-a-half years after physical birth the ether body frees itself from the head region, how in the following two-and-a-half years it frees itself from the chest region and finally, up to the change of teeth, from the child's metabolic and limb system.[10]

What might Steiner mean when speaking about an ether body that frees itself from the head region, from the chest region and finally, from the child's metabolic and limb system? Once a region is free, then that region's inherent forces and capacities come into play in a different form from that in which they existed previously. Although the sequence mentioned here occurs from the head down, that is not always the case.

In the case of the ether body of formative forces—the domain of the Cosmic Artist of Sculpture—the fact that it finishes first with the head region indicates that some of the finer formations of the brain, of the larynx, and of some of the sense organs are sculpted and near completion according to the requirements for this particular life for this particular individual.[11] A bit later, between two-and-a-half and five years of age, during the time when the ether body is working on the heart, lungs, and rhythmic system, the child opens itself to the next Cosmic Artist. Finally, during the last two-and-a-half years of its primary sculpting activity, the ether body finishes details of the limbs and the metabolic or digestive organs.

So the primary importance of the Cosmic Sculptor is to fine-tune the physical body, to ensure that all organs work the way they need to work to provide for the physical health of the incarnating human being. Anyone who observes carefully the growth of physical capacities, and also the concomitant awakening of mental capacities, will recognize, through direct observation, this fine-tuning activity of the ether body. Once the ether body has finished its tasks in the head region of the infant, then mental capacities of language and, particularly, memory become possible. Once the fine-tuning activity of the middle region of heart and lungs is accomplished, the possibility for more detailed memory pictures arises. And once the fine-tuning activity has been completed for the rest of the body, physical capacities of movement, endurance, and strength are enhanced.

When the ether body has touched on all internal organs, checking their function and their life-sustaining capacities, after the approximate age of seven, certain childhood illnesses may arise. Steiner discusses these childhood illnesses as crucial experiences for the awakening personality, in that, through these childhood diseases, hereditary traits may be discarded. The child begins to come into its own, assuming its own body as a tool of its own individuality. Vaccination and other medical intervention to prevent these childhood diseases, then, may be viewed as preventing the development of strong personalities.

The ether body, touching all parts of the physical body in sequence, enables a child to become a perfect imitator. (Steiner spoke of the achievements of the first three years, of the first deeds of physical existence—uprightness, language, and thinking—as given to human beings through the Christ.[12]) As adults, when we sculpt, we use the qualities of the ether body, its inherent imitative capacity, to bring our ideas to life. From classical sculpture up through recent times, the human body has been the main object of the sculptor. When, in the course of the twentieth century, sculptors began to make abstract sculptures, many individuals found these peculiar and inexpressive. We appreciate sculptures based on the human body because our ether body is an imitator, and we recognize universal human forms. Because of this imitative capacity, adults who work with, or spend time around, young children must act and speak morally.

> Therefore education during these first two-and-a-half years should be confined to the self-education of the adult in charge who should think, feel and act in a manner which, when perceived by the child, will cause it no harm.[13]

The apocryphal gospels mention an incident in which the Jesus child made twelve sparrows of clay on the Sabbath, made them live and fly forth. Such a story relates sculptural activity to life, to the ether body.

3. Picturing Capacities: The Cosmic Painter

Around the age of three, young children develop the capacity to picture inwardly what they experience and observe in their surroundings. This capacity, as is appropriate for the age, relies to a large extent on imitation. When young children play, they often imitate, or mimic, the adult world.

Three- and four-year-olds having a tea party in the sandpit, imitating the dog chasing a squirrel, imitating a bus driver or daddy driving the car, imitating mother cooking or father painting the house—all this imitation takes place when a child repeats the actions, deeds and words that adults use in performing their actions. These motions and words are usually very accurate copies of the adults' words and actions. Sometimes these are quite amusing, and often they are irritating to adults, who do not understand the need of these young children to instill what they observe into their own memories, and so strive, through their repetitive actions and words, to engrave visual and verbal memories ever more deeply. Through imitation, young children are practicing memory. When young children imitate their elders, they carry memory pictures away from the location of the actual occurrence, transplant the imaginary event to another location, and then continue to re-live, re-experience, re-construct, and thus re-member the event. They place themselves in the center of this living memory picture. In other words, they are able to have an inner picture, one that they carry with them.

This new capacity to picture the world around them may be attributed to the inspiration of the Cosmic Painter. His gift enables children from the age of three or so on to picture, in their minds and their souls, either a physical event or object or an imagined event or object. Dreams reveal a similar process—an often jumbled concoction of real events or objects thrown together with imagined events or objects. Young children often have vivid recurring dreams or nightmares at this age.

According to Steiner's description of the arts, the astral body—the movement and consciousness organization of the human being, an entirely non-physical part of the human makeup[14]—works into the life organization to express itself in the art of painting. A picture is not a reality. Artists, at least the great artists of the past, designed their paintings in accordance with the artistic traditions of their age in order to bring a particular content to the viewer. This content is an intention, living in the astral organization, that imprints itself into the life organization. This life organization of the human being, as of all living entities in nature, obeys laws in its functioning, experiencing rhythms in time and in space. The life organization is also related to the liquid element, to water. Consciousness working into a plane of liquid—that is the painter's art.[15]

The capacity to have visual memories enables a child, at a later stage of development, to pull or form precise memories from a flexible, one might say, fluid, pool of memory.[16] Young human beings begin to paint, as it were, into their fluid organization their memory pictures of observed events. Human understanding is intimately bound up with this memory pool. Throughout life, we rely on accurate memory capacities. We cannot learn to read, write, or do arithmetic without an accurate memory pool. The best preparation of young children, then, for later academic learning is to allow and encourage them to develop visual and aural memory through their natural tendency to imitate their environment. The environment, however, must be worthy of imitation. An environment immoral in action and attitude defiles the essence of humanity; young children will then imitate what will hinder their development into worthwhile members of humankind.

All learning from school age on requires this picture-forming capacity. Without it, the imagination of a child will not become active. With it, truly remarkable creations of imagination may take place.

4. Rhythm, Number, Voice, and Harmony: The Cosmic Musician

Steiner repeatedly discussed music in his pedagogical lectures. According to Steiner, the human astral body—the consciousness and movement organization of the human being—is built up primarily by musical elements, beginning in a child's seventh year:

> [C]ertain of these forces begin to work more in the child's soul and spiritual realm, affecting especially the rhythmical movement of heart and lungs. It [the child] has a real longing for this interplay of

rhythm and beat in its own organism. Consequently the adult must realize that whatever he or she brings to the child after the change of teeth, has to be given with an inherent quality of rhythm and beat... If, at this stage, the rhythm of breathing and blood circulation is not treated in the right way, the resulting harm may extend irreparably into later life. At this stage the child's muscles vibrate in sympathy with the rhythms of breathing and blood circulation, so that the entire being of the child takes on a musical character... [N]ow the inner musician begins to work, albeit beyond the child's consciousness.[17]

Music demonstrates a threefold division—rhythm and measure, harmony, and melody. The Cosmic Sculptor works down from the head, through the rhythmic system, and into the metabolism and limbs. By contrast, the Cosmic Musician, whose function is to establish the nervous system as servant of the human mind, as servant of an individual's will, feeling and thinking, works from the limbs and metabolism upward toward the head. As teachers, we are faced with the necessity to aid the development or perfection of the nerves of the limbs of a child from approximately seven to nine years of age. The first component of music, rhythm and measure, is of vital importance beginning roughly at age seven. Teaching must engage students appropriately with rhythm and measure. Rhythm and measure are best experienced through movement of the limbs. Fundamental facts of math, for example, may be memorized effectively via rhythmic movements. Every subject taught during the first years of elementary school needs to be taught, not in an abstract vacuum, but through engaging movement.

On a personal note: In 1975 I had the privilege as part of a year-long sabbatical from Michael Mount Waldorf School in Johannesburg, South Africa, to travel to many schools in Europe. In many locations I saw students even in Waldorf schools seated during main lessons, not moving, listening to the instructions of their teachers, but not experiencing the content of the lessons through their own movements. At that point I resolved to become a missionary of movement.

I further based my mission on the following teaching experience, inspired by Max Stibbe, a Waldorf school pioneer in South Africa. I began to teach primary subjects first of all through movement. I followed this with artistic and feeling-emotional expansion, and, finally, toward the end of a subject block, by stimulating intellectual conclusions. I practiced this for the elementary grades, although in the higher grades the movement portion became shorter. I intended to prove to myself that an initial experience of movement would form the basis for awakening the intellect, as Steiner describes.[18] I concluded that, indeed, when introducing subjects through movement, students are engaged, memory strengthened, and thinking capacities aroused.

During the second seven-year stage of development, the soul capacities of will, of feeling, and of thinking develop from their home in the human astral body. Still, music will help us best to guide our students.[19]

> If people work physically, they move their limbs. That means they swim totally immersed in the spirit. This is not the spirit dammed up in that person, it is the spirit outside. Rather, what is important is the extent to which people are purposefully active. Purposefully active— these words must permeate us if we are to teach children.[20]

Purposeful activity may include not only dance and eurythmy, but also the enactment of a usually abstract subject or process, such as arithmetic. It depends on the ingenuity of the teacher to transform such an abstract subject into a movement experience—so that education is experienced, enlivened.

Melody is, in its purest form, a single voice. A melody is like a sentence or a statement. Our inherent musical capacity enables us to complete a melody even if we hear only the first two or three bars. In this relation of melody and sentence we preview the work of the next Cosmic Artist.

The crisis that children may experience around the age of nine or ten is also a herald of the next Cosmic Artist. This crisis appears in the middle of the second seven-year stage when the melodic element is important. The crisis is due to a newly awakened capacity for critical discernment, and no one—not teacher, parent, classmates, other adults, or the world in general—is exempt from critical appraisal. This critical appraisal, moreover, is directed toward the child itself. The appearance of this capacity for critical appraisal signifies the awakening of self-experience, self-respect, and separation from the world at large. Parents and teachers need to understand this crisis as a vital step toward selfhood. Adult understanding of students in this transformative stage is essential because students expect adults to understand what they are undergoing. Because this awakening selfhood announces itself during the melodic stage, we can say that, from this age on, each individual is singing her or his own song. The full expression and potentiality of the new capacity will reveal itself only when we consider the next Cosmic Artist.

Social life becomes more important toward the end of the elementary school years when students' voices begin to change. Students begin to understand consciously working with others and the social context of their actions, feelings, and insights. Context—or harmony—becomes important during this last phase, approximately between twelve and fourteen years of age. This is also the stage at which students begin to gain intellectual understanding and begin to develop the rationality expected of adults.

Musical experience is, among other things, related to what Steiner often describes as the "outside" spiritual world, the world in which the planets are related in musical ratios, the harmony of the spheres, according to Kepler. In ancient times, the strings of lyres (I suspect also of other instruments) were tuned in such a way that the bass string was related to the earth element, the next string to the water element, the next string to the air element, and the last string to the fire element—thus linking music directly to the cosmos.[21] When we use music in our teaching or when we bring musical elements to subject matter in purposeful movement, we relate our students to the world, to the macrocosm, and to the world of the spirit around us.

5. Poetry and the Power of the Word: The Cosmic Poet

A human being is actually born four times. The first birth, physical birth, is obvious. The birth of the ether body, takes place around the change of teeth. The astral body—the movement or consciousness organization—is born at about fourteen years of age, and the ego—the eternal essence of an individual—is born at about twenty-one years of age. The first two births place a human being firmly on and into the physical world of earth, space, time, and nature, but the latter two are purely spiritual. They leave the earthly physical and ether bodies behind during sleep, for example, and experience purely spiritual events.

Around age nine, the human individuality turns or reorients itself. In the first years of life, when the physical and ether bodies are becoming established, a child is oriented toward the past—that is, toward past incarnations as well as toward her or his sojourn in spiritual worlds before birth. Around age nine, a change of direction, a turning toward the future takes place. From about the ninth year on, a child becomes alert to the physical world, enters more deeply than before into sensory experiences, begins to reason, and thus, by rejecting or affirming the world around in critical appraisal, begins to assert her- or himself. In other words, the individual now begins to experience her- or himself as the center of the present incarnation. We may picture this turnaround as a yin-yang figure, with the past coming into the center and the future radiating from it.

At this critical turning point comes the Cosmic Poet, or the Cosmic Word. Through the power of language and poetry, individual expression now becomes a possibility for the student. Aspects of grammar, writing, spelling, and reading may have been learned previously, but using language as a tool of individual expression, and thus becoming the creator of a new world, now becomes possible. Not every child is gifted enough to create poetry, to write potent stories of imagined events or retellings, or to write moving letters, but many do. As with the other Cosmic Artists, the Cosmic Poet endows the language a child uses with power. Individual circumstances determine how this power of language is taken up and utilized for individual expression.

One might also consider that the Cosmic Word is a power expressly manifest in human beings. While scientists may teach sign language to apes, and some animals may understand some words (or simply respond to the emotional essence), speech organs are unique to humanity. Language provides the uniquely human ability to create a commonality with other human beings, to understand and to be understood, to be social.

Human beings express their individuality in their particular language, and this gift is with them as they turn to the future, to how they will live this life, how they will bring their spiritual potentiality to physical expression. One example from the Waldorf school curriculum may help to illustrate this point. Fourth grade stories are often taken from Norse mythology. The stories of gods and giants, dwarfs and men are exciting! The story of the Norns who spin the lives of men is relevant as children confront their own destinies. The Norse myths may be used to teach the correct forms of past, present and future verbs. They can also yield recitations of alliterative poems, which emphasize repetitive sounds. These alliterative poems give teachers the opportunity to accompany recitation with strong movements. From movement and recitation through grammar to destiny, Norse myths relate the mundane and the cosmic for developing young children.

According to Steiner, whatever relates the human being to her or his higher senses, especially what expresses itself in the higher arts, is connected to the working of the time spirits—they work into our sense of hearing. While thinking, we are connected to the working of the archangels; when exercising our capacity of memory, we are permeated by the world of the angels; and when using our ego, our individuality, we make the fullest use of our physical body. Simply through the human constitution we are in continuous relationship to spiritual worlds.[22] It is crucial that human beings regain the consciousness that spiritual beings give the gifts of memory, intelligence, and sense perception, gifts that allow us to become truly human.

6. Dance and the Power of Building Community: The Cosmic Dancer

The next Cosmic Artist begins working on the adolescent around the age of fourteen. At that time it is essential that a young person learn to work with others. What better way to learn to adjust to others than to move together in a dance, in eurythmy. The success of a dance or drama depends on split-second timing; its enjoyment depends on a group-awareness; its satisfaction depends on the performers' social awareness. If students work together in practical and artistic endeavors in high school, they will develop a social conscience. The lack of this social conscience, unfortunately, is woefully obvious in today's youth worldwide. The emphasis on abstract, intellectual learning and the lack of conscious, artistic social work exacerbates this situation.

What does the Cosmic Dancer develop? The future quality of what Steiner calls the "life spirit" working into the individual, the "spirit self." At the present stage of human development, the life spirit is a distant promise, not yet a fact. It is a promise that the capacities of life-sustaining processes may be controlled, ordered, and directed by individuals themselves. The natural rhythms of life that develop when working with others in harmony may eventually transform into a capacity for guiding one's own life processes.

It will soon be essential that human beings demonstrate a social conscience. Today we are training for it; today's problems—social, economic, or political—provide the training ground; today, we are challenged to heed our social conscience. While materialism—and the egotism that results from it—provide challenges to the emergence of a social conscience, the practices of dance, eurythmy, and drama in the formative years from fourteen to twenty-one facilitate its development.

The human ego, working into the social fabric from about eighteen years of age, also develops as it works into the astral body in these years. In contrast to the astral body, which takes hold of the physical nerves along the paths of limbs, chest, and, finally, head, the ego begins with the head. Teenagers, through intellectual rationalizations, seem to be able to disprove everything that adults state. The self, as with the ether body, incarnates from the head downward, so logic lights up first, and with it the endless and provocative ratiocinations of adolescents. Then, in the middle years of this period, from about sixteen to eighteen, the battle for emotional equanimity begins. At this point it is crucial that the ship of the self is not wrecked by emotional insecurity, wild desires, or unattainable goals. Gradually, maturity of the feeling life, of the social conscience, has to be established for future well being, for future functioning in the adult world.

At this stage, adolescents are most at risk and highly influenced by the environment. They fight a battle for balance, which, for many individuals, continues into adult life. They must find the middle ground between fear and rage, between the bestial and the arrogant, for example.

The third phase of adolescence has to do with the application of the human will. Work in the larger community, in whatever form, helps expand the reach of individual will. It is a challenge to carry out what the self desires. Another challenge is to prepare for one's future, to picture oneself in a future profession, to find a star to follow. This phase begins at the end of high school, when adolescents begin seriously to consider their futures, and when role models become ever more important. High school teachers need to be and introduce worthy role models to their students as preparation for coming adulthood. In this way, young women and men prepare for the dance of life.

7. Who Are We? The Cosmic Self-Development Artist

During the years of adolescence the eternal self begins to mature in preparation for the earthly self, the ego, which is born at about twenty-one years of age. Fundamental questions arise in the middle years of adolescence: Who am I? What am I supposed to do in the world? What is my mission? What is my task? These questions may arise, largely unconsciously, well before the age of twenty-one. But now maturity raises the corollary question: How will I go about becoming who I want to be?

The twenties yield the possibility of acquiring knowledge and expertise but not yet the assurance and certainty that comes with maturity. Traditionally, learning takes place in universities and apprenticeships. While the self comes to a realization of him- or herself as a person active in the world at large, much fine-tuning is required during one's twenties. From twenty-one to twenty-eight years of age, the eternal self faces the challenge of permeating as fully as possible that part of the human soul which Steiner characterizes as the sentient soul—an extension of the astral body:

> The sentient soul not only receives the impressions of the outer world in the form of sensations but also has a life of its own that is fructified both by sensations from one side and by thinking from the other.[23]

Now thinking verifies the tasks that the eternal self chooses as its work in the world. Often, but not always, during these years we meet those who become our life teachers or mentors. The future beckons; training ceases; we begin to make our own lives. Our own goals become the star that guides us into the future.

Conclusion

The Cosmic Artists continue their work after our twenties, but now they work not as agents of bodily and soul development, but as agents of renewal and rejuvenation. We can experience this through the practice of their arts.

In his second lecture to those who would work with severely challenged children, Steiner explained that, through their own efforts, these teachers would be able to effect changes in those children whose fundamental organization is lacking, who are not able to progress in the same way or at the same pace as most other human beings. Steiner explained that, in order to further physical bodily development, a teacher's ether body should provide a healthful effect. To further the development of a student's ether body, a teacher's astral body should exert itself in self-development. In order to ameliorate what lives in a student's astral body, a teacher's ego must work on itself. And in order to have an effect on a student's ego, a teacher's spirit self—though not yet fully developed—is called upon. This spirit self often shows itself in all that lives in humanity at large as moral impulses.[24]

As adults, we may work on our own development and we may learn from each other. Something that is well developed in a friend, acquaintance, or co-worker may influence a part of us. Community develops in this way. And it is in this manner that the arts will have a healing and rejuvenating effect on human beings. The Seven Cosmic Artists, who help all children to develop toward their adult lives in the service of humanity, show us by their unwavering example that, as teachers and as parents, we help growing children when we strive to develop ourselves, using the gifts of spiritual worlds, to the best of our ability.

"The Seven Cosmic Artists: An Artistic View of Child Development" first appeared in the *Research Bulletin*, Vol. XI, No. 2, Spring, 2006.

ENDNOTES

1. Steiner, Rudolf. *The Arts and Their Mission*, Lecture 8, Oslo, May 20, 1923, CW 276, Spring Valley, NY: Anthroposophic Press, 1964.

2. Steiner, Rudolf. *Art in the Light of Mystery Wisdom,* CW 275, London: Rudolf Steiner Press, 1970.

3. I have lectured about this particular description of child development, but these ideas are presented here in writing for the first time.

4. Steiner, Rudolf. *Soul Economy and Waldorf Education*, particularly Chapters 7 and 9, CW 303, Spring Valley, NY: Anthroposophic Press, 1986.

5. See below regarding artistic impulses related to the heart-lung rhythmic system.

6. We do not disregard the role of genetics. But scientists themselves have doubted that genetics alone determines the form, the morphology, of living beings. See, for instance, Weihs, Thomas J. *Embryogenesis in Myth and Science*, Edinburgh: Floris Books, 1986.

7. Steiner, Rudolf. *Man's Being, His Destiny and World Evolution*, Lecture of May 17, 1923, CW 226, Spring Valley, NY: Anthroposophic Press, 1952.

8. Third grade students in Waldorf schools, when learning about houses and buildings, often recognize that buildings are like human bodies.

9. Steiner, Rudolf. *The Apocalypse of St. John*, CW 104, Chapter 9, London: Rudolf Steiner Press, 1977.

10. Op. cit., Steiner. *Soul Economy,* Lecture 7.

11. Young children clearly see, hear, and experience their surroundings differently than adults do; for instance, many young children have invisible companions.

12. Steiner, Rudolf, *The Spiritual Guidance of the Individual and Humanity*, CW 15, Hudson, NY: Anthroposophic Press, 1974.

13. Op. cit., Steiner. *Soul Economy*.

14. For detailed descriptions of the parts of a human being, see Steiner, Rudolf. *Theosophy,* CW 9, Anthroposophic Press, 1994.

15. In the first book of the Bible, *Genesis,* the Spirit of God hovers over the waters.

16. See also Steiner, Rudolf. *The Destinies of Individuals and of Nations*, Lecture of March 16, 1915, CW 157, London: Rudolf Steiner Press, 1986.

17. Op. cit., Steiner. *Soul Economy,* Lecture 9.

18. Steiner, Rudolf. *Foundations of Human Experience*, Lecture 11, Hudson, NY: Anthroposophic Press, 1996.

19. I have described these techniques in two of my other books, *The Temperaments and the Arts* and *Awakening Intelligence*, both published by AWSNA Publications.

20. Steiner, Rudolf. *Foundations of Human Experience*, Lecture 13, Great Barrington, MA: SteinerBooks, 1996.

21. Paraphrased from Steiner, Rudolf. *Occult Signs and Symbols*, Lecture of December 28, 1907, CW 101, New York: Anthroposophical Press, 1972.

22. Paraphrased from Rudolf Steiner. *Spiritual and Social Transformations in the Course of the Development of Humanity*, Lecture of February 13, 1920, CW 196 (currently untranslated).

23. Op. cit., Steiner. *Theosophy*, Chapter 1.

24. Steiner, Rudolf. *Education for Special Needs*, Lecture 2, CW 317, London: Rudolf Steiner Press, 1998.

Mathematics:
Quotations, Questions and Comments

I do not know what the situation is in Europe today at the beginning of the twenty-first century. In America, however, in public education and in private schools, it seems that the methods of teaching math are, on the whole, ineffective. However, in American public schools it is often the children of Asian immigrants who excel in math. Why? A second riddle: The methodology applied in Waldorf schools for teaching seems to work well. In this essay I shall look at some of Steiner's comments about teaching mathematics and attempt to solve some questions that arise concerning the nature of mathematics.

> These so-called scientific, geometrical, arithmetical, algebraic and movement representations cannot be applied to external experiences which are based on what we have gained from the external world, but the former arise from within us, they really do not correspond to ideas that we experience externally. These former ideas arise from our own intelligence, they arise from the intelligent part of our will, of the will part of our soul. There is a tremendous difference between all other representations in our arena of intelligence and those deriving from geometrical, arithmetical and movement representations. All other representations we derive from experiences of the external world; these geometrical, arithmetical and movement ideas arise from the unconscious part of the will, having an external organ in our metabolism.[1]

The Intelligent Part of the Will

Steiner describes the soul life of all individuals as consisting of will, feeling and thinking capacities. While he assigns each part of the soul life a home in the human body—thinking with the human head, feeling with the human chest and torso, and the will part associated with both the metabolism and the limbs in general—he also states that in each portion of the human body thinking, feeling and will express themselves in particular formations. Consequently the question arises, just where can we find the intelligent part of the human will?

We find help in Steiner's statement as quoted above, namely the mention of the *movement representations* together with the mathematical, algebraic and geometrical representations. One could say, there seem to be inherent in some individuals the capacity to predict accurately exactly their relation to three-dimensional space, for example, athletes in the performance of their feats.

While watching them, who has not been astonished by the remarkable feats of some athletes? At the extraordinary capacity to control their movements; at the agility of moving into the exact positions needed to carry out their objectives; at the apparently unconscious wisdom of these actions? And they are often not even aware of what they are doing! It seems to be an unconscious, possibly instinctual capacity towards the correct action.

I suggest that this capacity, as it manifests in athletes, is present in all human beings. Agility, dexterity, nimbleness and alertness are all expressions of the intelligent part of the will. In this way, the metabolic-limb organization lives out in human movement capacities. Granted, this capacity is not always developed to its greatest potential. But might this be one reason why the children of Asian immigrants to America often excel in math? They are more agile?

One could further suggest that when one can align himself so well to his physical surroundings, then he is able to predict the outcome of his own and also of other individual's actions by simply being in such harmony with his environment. However, is there a possibility that this capacity of athletes can be primed and trained? It should be apparent that all sports activities involve extensive training which provides for enhancing the motions of athletes in three-dimensional space, enhancing speed and ability, and so strengthening and working together with other players in team effort and accomplishment. Could we consider this as what Howard Gardner refers to as *movement intelligence*?[2]

While I have taken this example of athletic ability relating to wisdom of movement, in many Waldorf schools athletic training is not begun until the upper grades. One should not confuse such athletic abilities with excellence in mathematics. However, some individuals may exhibit remarkable capacities, which demonstrates what Steiner indicated in the above quotation, but do not demonstrate athletic capacities as a precursor to excellence in mathematics. Other abilities need to be developed and are also inherent for this occurrence.

Do Waldorf schools consider this athletic capacity as a precursor for mathematical intelligence? Not at all. However, many exercises done often in the lower grades of a Waldorf school (for instance, those often referred to as *body geography*) help lead to the kind of mental agility, combined with physical alertness and nimbleness, which supports mathematical capacities.

The important and valid relationship of individuals to three-dimensional space is the agent that elicits the intelligent part of the will, not athletic ability per se. Consequently, in the early grades of Waldorf education, there is a strong emphasis on the exercises for physical agility and dexterity, also spatial movements which call forth the relationship with three-dimensional space. Through these actions the students stimulate the intelligent part of the will. One particular aspect of this has to do with the transference of spatial motion and patterns into more abstract representations, such as pictures and images. For instance, if students are asked to draw what they have just executed a moment ago in movement activity, in a kind of diagram, then this is an important factor in asserting the intelligent part of the will in a symbolic manner. In mathematics we have a great deal of symbolism, both with notation, as well as with numerical values. When students practice transferring movement patterns which they have experienced into graphic representations, then the rightfully abstract, that is fully mental, way of working with mathematics is strengthened.

Comment: I have several times had the opportunity to work with individual students who have shown some problems dealing with the math of the early grades. I have demonstrated to my satisfaction, and also to their teachers and parents, that working consistently with all aspects of three-dimensional space in movement exercises helps stimulate mathematical abilities.

Steiner compares mathematical concepts with all other concepts and states that in all other concepts, particularly those related to the higher senses, either visual or tonal aspects are primary, but perhaps not readily apparent to casual inspection.

But there is one kind of concept with which you cannot do this [relate it to a tonal or visual element], as you will soon see. You cannot do it in the realm of mathematical concepts. Insofar as they are purely mathematical, there is no trace of the tonal or the visible. The basis of these pure mathematical concepts is not related to the seen or the heard, but it relates itself in the last analysis to our will impulse. There is an unfolding of action around three angles as shown by the motion of the hand or by walking, by turning of the body. What you have within you as a will-concept is in reality what you carry into the pure mathematical concept. You can distinguish the inner compelling nature of mathematical concepts from the merely empirical or non-compelling nature of other concepts. This distinction arises from the fact that mathematical concepts are so closely bound up with our own selves that we carry our will nature into them. Only what we experience in the sphere of the will is brought into mathematical operations.[3]

No tonal or visual elements are related to obviously inherent mathematical concepts. Steiner states that mathematical concepts are expressly *not* related to the higher senses (Word, Thought, Ego or the perception of another human being in possession of a self), which contain some visual or tonal elements.

Mathematical Concepts Inherent in Human Bodies

Might Steiner be referring to the lower senses in the above quotation as opposed to the higher senses?[4] What is it about the senses of Touch, Well-Being (or Life), Movement and Balance (these are termed the lower senses by Steiner), that relate to mathematical concepts? Or is there a relationship? Let us take a closer look.

When an infant within the first weeks of life begins to experience touch, she or he begins to distinguish her- or himself as an entity separate from the environment. Later in the first year of life the sense of Well-Being is apparent in smiling or weeping, as the case may be, through bodily events. Later still the sense of Movement supports crawling, and so distinguishes different body motions for moving forward, back or sideways in space. Finally, the sense of Balance enables the infant to right her- or himself and begin to look freely into three-dimensional space. One might refer to the bodily efforts during the first year of life as the beginning orientation into three-dimensional space in an unconscious, instinctual manner.

Could the experience of these four lower senses be instrumental for developing an inherent sense of numbers, of mathematics? And what about the practice today of many parents putting their infants into jumpers or walkers? They miss out on having to learn to crawl, sit, turn or become upright! Might these practices undermine the development of mathematical thinking? In any event, let us analyze the respective lower senses in relationship to some mathematical concepts.

The *Sense of Touch* provides for each individual the direct experience that she or he is an independent entity. Young children, when counting or learning to count, often touch the objects they are counting (or use their fingers to count). Counting as a capacity seems to be related to the sense of touch. It is significant that during the first grader's introduction in a Waldorf school to numbers counting is often done as marching and stomping, with one step for each number, and thus emphatically touching the floor.

The *Sense of Well-Being* (or *Life*) tells the individual how well his metabolism is working, or not working. In the case of an infant, hunger or other activity of his or her metabolism causes the infant to cry or smile. The persistence of these metabolic urges parallels the persistence of certainty in respect of math problems. The working metabolism has to actually activate addition, subtraction, division and multiplication through its activity of uniting or separating from it the external foods and other substances and forces, and sending them to different parts of the body. (I am not going to go into which metabolic elements are responsible for which arithmetical function. I leave this to the ingenuity of each teacher.) We might see in the activation of this metabolism the original capacity of the human body to engage in the four arithmetical processes. I am aware of the fact that this is a somewhat strange thought; however it might be a valid idea for first grade teachers to picture these four processes in relation to human metabolism.

The *Sense of Movement* enables the infant to juxtapose her or his limbs when moving about. It has inherently to do with purposefully engaging in specific positions, towards a specific goal. When we solve problems in arithmetic, we need to see clearly what the problem is and then arrange its elements so that they lead us to the solution—in other words, we need to grasp the position of the problem. In this way we actually put these elements side by side as if we were crawling in early childhood. This is, for instance, very important regarding word problems. Difficult problems need to be clearly stated, and in these clear statements the juxtaposing of their elements should make the solution apparent, or at least the path towards the solution. Just as the sense of movement informs the body how to position limbs in order to move forward or back, the sense of movement can help inform the student how to state a problem clearly and move forward to its solution.

The *Sense of Balance* helps ensure an individual's standing upright to face the world. Mathematically that might mean that we are able to face each problem with confidence that a solution will be found. The sense of balance will also play itself out in the math of the higher grades, when dealing with area, volume, and equations as to the actuality of the world. It means that a certain sense of complexity will allow the individual to *see* the path towards a solution.

In the math curriculum of the grade school, there are many parallels to the metabolic relationships of the body as a whole. The relationship between the lower senses and the fundamental arithmetic problems of the grades might seem fanciful, but could lead to insights useful for a teacher.

> Why is it that we can count in the first place? We can actually count by means of the etheric body; in reality, a number is still nothing but a comparison with what is contained within us. The whole of arithmetic is in us; we brought it to birth within us through our astral body. It actually emerges from our astral body, our ten fingers being merely replicas of the astral and etheric. These two are only utilized by the external fingers, whereas, when we do sums, we express in the etheric body what brings about the inspiration of numbers in the astral body; then we count by means of the etheric body, with which we think in the first place. Therefore, we can say that, outwardly, counting is something quite abstract for us today; inwardly, the reason we count is connected with the fact that we are counted in the first place, for we are counted out of universal being and are structured according to numbers. Numbers are inborn into us, woven into us out of cosmic totality. Within ourselves, each number has its own definite quality.[5]

It is not surprising that in the first grade of a Waldorf school, when the students are introduced to numbers, they are also introduced to a qualitative number experience. With this qualitative experience, which Steiner delineates further in the above-quoted lecture, aspects of former evolutionary epochs of humanity are revisited, for example, when a *three* showed a different quality than a *two*. The inner quality of a number was experienced right into the sheaths of a human being.

Where Is the Essence of Numbers Lodged?

We should ask ourselves what meaning we may give to the ether and astral bodies in respect to number. Let us consider first these terms in their original meaning, without considering them in respect to the essence of number.

When discussing the astral body of a human being (not in respect to animals, who also have this astral body), Steiner describes this constituent of the human being as the *soul body*, that within us that carries out the various soul functions, such as feeling and the will nature, as well as our thinking capacities. Steiner frequently refers to these forces of the human soul as cosmic forces, related to the zodiac, for instance. These functions give human beings the vigor and motivation to actually engage in action. At the beginning of this essay we quoted a reference by Steiner delineating arithmetic with the *thinking part of the will nature* of human beings. But in regard to the astral body and astral forces, they provide the possibility for external activity. It is through the capacities of our astral bodies that we actually are able to act whenever our self (or ego) decides to do so. This self or ego, the eternal human entity, is quite close to the astral body and controls it to a limited extent. This control is actually what individuals in our age are supposed to master. Steiner refers to the astral part of human nature as being a foundation for numbers, as all activity towards dealing with numbers needs to become energized by our astral capacities, or our inner soul life.

Steiner describes astral bodies, and also etheric (or ether) bodies, as auras surrounding the form of the physical body.[6] These may be seen as form and energy fields that individuals who have an ability to see auras may perceive, but that for most individuals in our particular stage of human evolution are invisible, although they may be detected by their effects.

The ether body has a different configuration than the astral body. It is intimately connected with all aspects that bestow and maintain life in human beings and in all other parts of nature. While the astral configuration exhibits all the soul functions of a human being, the ether body indicates that human beings are alive. The ether configuration also imitates closely the physical body. Human beings have this living entity in common with all other living entities in nature. The forces active in this living entity are not earthly, but cosmic forces. Forces from our solar system in particular energize their corresponding forces within us. As we gaze out into the night sky to admire the sparkling stars, we are reminded that the origin of all life is from the cosmos, not from the earth, although the earth provides a home for human beings and all of nature. Such life forces in the human body regulate a number of different functions.

One aspect of the ether body needs to be stated clearly in respect to arithmetic, the human capacity to be able to picture inwardly what we can observe externally. This inner picturing capacity is intimately connected to our ether body. It manifests often in our souls as the exciting imagery of dreams. While dreams are often fanciful, and we do not experience them as external reality, we are often moved by their imagery. We experience this quality of making images also in all the arts, through descriptive, fanciful and symbolic images. Our ether bodies give human beings the capacity to form images, and also the images we picture in our minds as a basis for external formation.

Working with number in all its forms, these capacities become possible through the fabric of our ether bodies. We may state quite boldly that all individuals who have mastered mathematics in any way must also have the possibility to imagine in picture form, or in idea form, what their formulae tell them. If there ever existed a mathematician who worked only in the abstract, not forming pictures, images or mental representations of his mathematical ideas, then it would be very difficult for such a person to actually present his ideas to others. Human beings who are not experienced in mathematics need to employ the image-making capacity in order to understand what a person is attempting to elucidate. This is easier to engage when there is a visual element to the presentation or discussion.

Initially this may seem to contradict what Steiner emphatically asserts that only in respect of the higher senses is there a tonal or visual element present. The capacity, however, to transform an idea into a picture is a capacity of the soul and relates directly to what Steiner describes as the sense of thought, which forms the image of an idea. Therefore, the sequence in the communication of mathematical ideas is such: first an individual has an idea, which she or he transforms within her or his soul into a picture; then this picture or idea is shared with others. Now, among mathematicians, this may not be necessary because they are so involved in the subject matter and so experienced that, upon hearing a mathematical idea, they can often form a picture of it immediately and translate this picture into practical applications. However, when mathematical ideas are to be communicated to those who are not trained in mathematics, then these ideas need to be translated into tangible, external images.

So if we are to teach mathematics to those who do not have a mathematical experience, then we have to understand these ideas so thoroughly that we are able to form images, and then can describe these images in a way those others can grasp. For example, when I was teaching seventh graders the Theorem of Pythagoras, I had to have a very clear idea in mind which preliminary geometrical constructions had to be verified— by walking them and also drawing them, by proving them in practice—so that when I introduced the elements of the Theorem of Pythagoras, the students would be able to "get it." I had to carefully work out the sequence of experiences that the students needed to have. It became apparent to me that lower grades students (from first through eighth grade) need to experience ideas in three-dimensional space, in order to internalize them and so come to understand them. Indeed, this holds good not only for mathematical ideas, but for others, too.

So we have before us: The ordinary outer empirical knowledge of nature, then mathematical knowledge, and finally, spiritual knowledge. We have, as the last step, through an inwardly creative activity, spiritual worlds before us. As preparation for viewing these worlds as real, we start by creating mathematical, pictorially-abstract elements. We use this mathematics in relation to the outer world, but if we are honest we must say: What we construct mathematically is still not a reality in itself; it does not bring reality up out of the depths of our souls, rather it is a picture of reality. In spiritual science we gain the ability to bring out of the depths of our souls what is not just a picture of the outer existence, but reality itself, true reality. The three levels of human knowledge are: knowledge of physical nature, mathematical knowledge and spiritual knowledge.[7]

Concerning oneself with mathematics, as well as teaching its fundamentals, one must begin by working actively in one's own soul. The pictorial-practical management of mathematical ideas, which are generated in one's soul, is proof of this. Imagine an architect who does not first picture the buildings he wishes to build! First the imagination, then the careful technical and mathematical work that needs to be done!

Mathematical Knowledge as Training for the Soul

For the teacher to work with all aspects of mathematics is a truly fundamental area of training one's imagination, training one's inner picturing capacities. These inner picturing capacities are also used in professional fields such as architecture, engineering and various other design modes of work.

And for students, mathematics is an equally vital training for inner picturing capacities, which are lacking in today's world, and are of great importance to our future world. It is crucial for the future of humanity that a shift in society is envisaged, for only when we are able to picture a future can we gain confidence and trust in this future and put our whole will to work on it. It is the students who will carry forward the future of human evolution. Therefore they should be able to make use of their best gifts towards it, including the intelligent part of the will. As Waldorf teachers we must strive to make good use of it in ourselves and help develop it in our students.

Now we can turn to the question of why mathematical work and knowledge in the Western world is so lacking. In general, humanity in the Western world has become very lazy, indolent in applying their natural talents. Further there is real concern mounting in the world of medicine today about the physical inactivity among school children, for instance— knowing what we know about the relationship of physical activity with mathematical abilities, we should make a serious effort to free the physical body to allow for its inherent talents for mathematics. Physical activity not only frees mathematical ability, but also increases confidence and certainty in moving about the world at large.

Perhaps this is the reason that the children of Asian immigrants often excel in math, for it is part of the cultural heritage to be able to move with agility and dexterousness. As teachers, we should do our best to help students develop mathematical thinking, because mathematics is on the border between natural science and spiritual science. It trains the inner life of human beings; it provides order, even in an abstract manner, but substantiated in the external, practical world through professional applications; it leads to inner activity by developing imagination.

Some Comments about Helping Students Gain Confidence in Mathematics

In summary, working with all aspects of three-dimensional space is essential. The teacher with imagination and ingenuity can develop challenging and varied forms and sequences for practice, including helping the students represent graphically what they have experienced in activity. When teaching aspects of mathematics, the following points should be kept in consideration:

- Mathematical thinking is intimately connected with awareness of three-dimensional space; consequently, all exercises that sharpen this awareness in any form, sequence, manner, and so forth, are beneficial. It is not enough to imagine such practices mentally, abstractly. It is vital to actually employ the human body directly in the actual doing, thus stimulating agility, dexterousness, physical nimbleness, and so forth. Once an exercise is completed, review it mentally, and thereby help the students integrate the concepts it conveys.

- Recording one's experiences in visual form brings consciousness to what one has carried out and adds to the details of one's experience. To conceptualize these experiences helps the student integrate and re-member.

- It is counterproductive in my opinion to attempt to explain to students why a particular procedure works. Rather, it is advantageous to encourage students to simply go ahead and apply a certain formula or process, for instance when learning to work with fractions in fourth grade. Then, through the actual working with fractions, the students grow to understand why this formula or that solves fractions problems. Action, even in just following a set course, activates students' understanding. Mathematics is based on the thinking part of the will, not on abstract understanding but on doing.

- When students begin to think logically, after the sixth grade, then understanding should come before undertaking mathematical work.

- Physical agility and motility of the students' bodies will have a good effect on their eventual understanding of everything that is connected with mathematical and geometrical thinking.

Again, mathematics, geometry, spatial considerations, and dexterous movements in three-dimensional space will not only increase mathematical understanding, but also serve to help individuals to develop inner certainty and inner life.

It is not for nothing that Plato demanded of his pupils that they must first of all have a good grounding in the knowledge of geometry and mathematics. Plato did not require an arithmetical or geometric knowledge of some particular kind, but rather a sound understanding of what really happens in a man when he does mathematics or geometry. This is based on a seemingly paradoxical but deeply meaningful saying of Plato: "God geometrizes." He did not mean by this that God just creates with mathematics five- or six-sided figures. Rather, He creates with the force of which we can only make pictures to ourselves, in our mathematical abstract thinking. Therefore I believe that he who understands the place of mathematics in the whole field of the sciences will also understand the correct place of spiritual science.[8]

ENDNOTES

1. Paraphrased from Rudolf Steiner, *The First Scientific Course about Light*, GA 320, Lecture of January 3, 1920.

2. Gardner, Howard. *Frames of Mind: The Theory of Multiple Intelligences*, 1983, as cited by Robert J. Sternberg in his *Metaphors of Mind*, Cambridge University Press, 2003.

3. Steiner, Rudolf. *Warmth Course*, Lecture of March 5, 1920, Spring Valley, NY: Mercury Press, 1988.

4. Steiner describes the human being as having twelve senses. *The Riddle of Humanity*, London: Rudolf Steiner Press, 1990.

5. Steiner, Rudolf. *Materialism and the Task of Anthroposophy*, GA 204, Lecture of April 23, 1921, New York: Anthroposophic Press, 1987.

6. Steiner, Rudolf. *How to Know Higher Worlds*, Anthroposophic Press, 1994, and *An Outline of Esoteric Science*, New York: Anthroposophic Press, 1997.

7. Steiner, Rudolf. *Anthroposophy and Science: Observation, Experiment, and Mathematics*, Spring Valley, NY: Mercury Press, 1991.

8. Ibid.

Bibliography

Auer, Arthur. *Learning about the World through Modeling*, Fair Oaks, CA: AWSNA Publications, 2002.

Howard, Michael. *Educating the Will*, Fair Oaks, CA: AWSNA Publications, 2002.

Lissau, Magda. *Awakening Intelligence*, Fair Oaks, CA: AWSNA Publications, 2004.

_____. *The Temperaments and the Arts*, Fair Oaks, CA: AWSNA Publications, 2003.

Steiner, Rudolf. *The Bridge between Universal Spirituality and the Physical Constitution of Man*, Spring Valley, NY: Anthroposophic Press, 1979.

_____. *Discussions with Teachers*, London: Rudolf Steiner Press, 1983.

_____. *Factors of Healing for the Social Organism*, Dornach, Switzerland: Goetheanum Verlag, 1969.

_____. *The Fall of the Spirits of Darkness*, Bristol, England: Rudolf Steiner Press, 1993.

_____. *Foundations of Human Experience*, Hudson, NY: Anthroposophic Press, 1996.

_____. *From Symptom to Reality in Modern History*, London: Rudolf Steiner Press, 1976.

_____. *Intuitive Thinking as a Spiritual Path*, Hudson, NY: Anthroposophic Press, 1995.

_____. *Practical Advice to Teachers*, London: Rudolf Steiner Press, 1976.

_____. *A Psychology of Body, Soul and Spirit*, Hudson, NY: Anthroposophic Press, 1999.

_____. *The Riddle of Humanity*, London: Rudolf Steiner Press, 1990.

_____. *Soul Economy and Waldorf Education*, London: Rudolf Steiner Press, 1986.

_____. *The Spiritual Ground of Education*, GA 305, New York: SteinerBooks, 2004.

_____. *The Spiritual Guidance of the Individual and of Humanity*, Hudson, NY: Anthroposophic Press, 1991.

_____. *Toward Imagination, Culture and the Individual*, Hudson, NY: Anthroposophic Press, 1990.

Usher, Stephen, ed. *Social and Political Science, An Introductory Reader*, Forest Row, England: Rudolf Steiner Press, 2003.

Strauss, Michaela. *Understanding Children's Drawings*, translated by Pauline Wehrle, London: Rudolf Steiner Press, 1978.